GODS
HELP

FOR
THE

TROUBLED
HEART

ED TAYLOR

GOD'S HELP
FOR THE
TROUBLED HEART

ED TAYLOR

GOD'S HELP FOR YOUR TROUBLED HEART

Copyright © 2020 by Ed Taylor

Library of Congress Cataloging-in-Publication Data

Names: Taylor, Ed

Title: God's Help for Your Troubled Heart

ISBN 978-0-9965723-1-6 paperback

Printed in the United States of America

www.calvaryCO.church

www.edtaylor.org

DEDICATION

To my wife Marie and kids, Joshua and Caitlin.
In memory of our son and brother Eddie and for his son Levi
(#onedaylittleguy) ... It was Eddie's sudden death that launched
our family into deep seasons of grief and pain. Grief was the place
where the Lord spoke to us in wonderful ways and birthed the
messages that became this book. Thank you!

Thank you to my assistant Cassandra, who tirelessly worked
behind the scenes to make this book into a reality.

Thank you to the fellowship family of Calvary Church,
whose love and support mean so much to us.

CONTENTS

INTRODUCTION

No one really sets out to write a book on suffering—no one hopes to live a life marked by suffering either. That's for a lot of reasons, I suppose. Life often takes us places we don't want to go. We don't always get to choose the type of book we will write.

Just because you love Jesus and serve Him, doesn't mean you won't experience pain, trials, or tragedy. The Christian doesn't get a pass on the difficulties of life. They come to us all—to those who believe in Jesus and those who don't. The only difference between us is faith. Faith in Jesus adds hope: Hope during the trial, and hope for the future.

As I write this, it's been just over five years since my wife and I experienced the deepest wound a parent can receive. Our twenty-six-year-old son Eddie, born to us as teenage parents, went home to His Savior after a valiant battle for life. His life ended much too early. My wife Marie and I joined the club no parent wants to be in. His brother and sister lost their friend. His son lost more than he could ever imagine. Loss. So much pain and loss surrounded Eddie's fight for life and the end-of-life decisions made for him.

W. Clement Stone said, "Big doors swing on little hinges." But on the fateful day of Eddie's death, our lives turned on a large hinge. Life would never be the same. Added to our family in large measure was a deep grief, debilitating depression, betrayal, tears, regret and a whole host of horrific events that were uninvited and unexpected—especially on the heels of our son's death.

We started asking questions we had really never asked before. The biggest question of course was, "Why?" God graciously never answered that question. There were other questions too: *Are all the things I've taught about being a Christian still true? Do I still believe them?*

Of course, time and time again, we found ourselves answering with a resounding yes. *Yes, I believe, but Lord help my unbelief!* God really does work all things together for the good, even when—no, especially when—we can't see it yet.

What emerged over the past few years in our tightly-knit family has been a resilient faith in a faithful God. At each stage, in each season, God has revealed Himself in strength and majesty. John reminds us, "If we are faithless, He remains faithful; He cannot deny Himself" (2 Tim. 2:13). It's true. Unfortunately, one of the only ways to know this with great certainty is to experience God's faithfulness for yourself. Grief will surely undermine your faith, or at least attempt to, almost daily.

In your hands is a series of truthful reminders of God's help for your troubled heart. He loves you. He wants to restore to you the hope you've lost though deep pain and tragedy. Listen, each of us have our stories of pain to share. But if we're not careful, we will refuse to accept and receive the healing Jesus so readily gives. Instead of living out stories of pain, God invites us to live in His redemptive story, full of faith and His faithfulness.

I didn't set out to write a book on suffering. It snuck up on me not too many years ago. I invite you to join me on a journey to healing through the Word of God, a journey I'm still on.

CHAPTER 1

GOD IS NOT FINISHED YET

No doubt, if you've experienced any type of suffering and pain in your life, you've asked the question, "Why?" Some parts of life feel so unfair, don't they? It doesn't matter whether you're asking because you feel you deserve better or because you want to believe there's purpose in your pain. Suffering has a way of drawing that question out of us all. We are hurting. We are confused. We are in pain.

And we want to know, "Why?"

I'm so sorry for the hurt you've experienced. The truth is trials, struggles, and difficulties are a part of this life. Bad things happen to good people. Bad things happen to bad people. Trials come to us all no matter our gender, ethnicity, age, or status in life. On this side of heaven—pain makes us all equals. None of us will escape the planet untouched.

Everything Is Vanity

The Bible tells the story of a man named King Solomon. He was the son of David, the same David who slew the giant Goliath and later became king of Israel. Solomon was the wisest and wealthiest man who ever lived. He had everything we could possibly want and more—wisdom, prestige, money, possessions, and power. But nothing satisfied him. In the book of Ecclesiastes, he famously wrote, "'Vanity of vanities,' says the Preacher; 'Vanity of vanities, all is vanity'" (Eccles. 1:2). In other words, It's all empty! Completely meaningless!

If you've been touched by trials, you know it's true. No one cares what kind of car they drive when they've lost someone they love. No one remembers how good their hair looked on the day everything went up in flames. Those things are meaningless. Empty. Vanity.

Solomon concludes the book of Ecclesiastes by summarizing what the man who had everything thought was most important: "Let us hear the conclusion of the whole matter: Fear God and keep His commandments, for this is man's all" (Eccles. 12:13).

Solomon had the unique perspective of someone who had everything this world could possibly offer. He had it all. Most of us will never experience that kind of wealth or opulence. When we're struggling, it's tempting to think, *If I only had [. . .], things would be better.* But it isn't true. Nothing this world has to offer can fill the ache of a devastated soul. In the book of Proverbs, Solomon wrote, "There are three things that are never satisfied, Four never say, 'Enough!': The grave, The barren womb, The earth that is not satisfied with water—And the fire never says, 'Enough!'" (Prov. 30:15b-16)

Why, God?

Unfortunately, many of us—Christians especially—feel this question so familiar to us all, is wrong. That God is offended when you ask Him, "Why?" *Why is this happening in my life? Why do I have to go through this? Why?* God is not offended by your questions. He is with you in your struggles and your pain.

In the book of Psalms, the psalmist cried out, "Behold, these are the ungodly, who are always at ease; They increase in riches. Surely I have cleansed my heart in vain, And washed my hands in innocence. For all day long I have been plagued, and chastened every morning"

(Ps. 73:12-14). He's hurting! He doesn't understand why wicked people seem to have it easy, while he's been doing the right thing with nothing to show for it.

In the book of Judges, Gideon questioned the angel of the LORD. "O my lord, if the Lord is with us, why then has all this happened to us? And where are all His miracles which our fathers told us about, saying, 'Did not the Lord bring us up from Egypt?'" (Judges 6:13) He doesn't understand why the same God who led them out of Egypt with mighty miracles would allow the Midianites to attack Israel, destroying their crops and leaving them with nothing.

You may be feeling the same way. You're not alone.

You may have been taught falsely that as a Christian, nothing bad will ever happen to you. You've been told, or you believed if you do the right thing—good things will happen. God will bless you. You will be happy, healthy, and wise. Life with Jesus means never having to suffer again. This is false. In fact, the Bible teaches the opposite. There will be trials. Sometimes more so because you are a Christian.

Perhaps you've heard all bad things are from the devil. If bad things are happening, you've sinned or you're under attack. It's all from the devil. You must not have enough faith, otherwise God would deliver you. This type of bad theology hurts people who are already hurting. It puts unnecessary pressure on desperate people to be more and do more. To *believe* more. And it's simply not true.

A Future Hope

In contrast to what Solomon discovered to be true of the world, the Bible teaches that *in Jesus*, everything is precious and wonderful. In Romans 8:28, the apostle Paul tells us, "And we know that all things work together for good to those who love God, to those who are the called according to His purpose." But that's hard to hear in the midst of suffering, isn't it? *God is able to take this—even this—and work it together in Jesus for my good?*

Notice Paul doesn't tell us all things are good. They aren't! If you've experienced storms, you know not everything that happens is good! The things the world offers to numb your pain are empty. But God is able to take those bad things and work them together for your good *in Jesus*. Everything in Jesus truly is precious and wonderful. In Him, you have everything you need to get through the storm.

In the book of Jeremiah, we find a message from God for the exiles in Jerusalem. Jeremiah lived during one of the darkest times in the nation of Israel's history. Israel had been defeated and conquered by the Babylonians. The majority of the Israelites were marched off into captivity in Babylon under the rule of Nebuchadnezzar. Only the poor were left to tend the fields of Jerusalem. Jeremiah was among those left behind. The people were broken, starving, and without hope. They saw no end in sight. In the midst of this terrible time God spoke to them. "'For I know the thoughts that I think toward you,' says the Lord, 'thoughts of peace and not of evil, to give you a future and a hope'" (Jer. 29:11). God's plan for you is good. He wants to give you a future and a hope. He sees you. He cares for you. He loves you.

The Hall of Faith in Hebrews 11 tells the stories of more than fifteen men and women who lived their lives by faith in spite of adversity. We tend to look at these men and women as heroes—and they are! But they were also just like you and me: they experienced trials, struggled through debilitating fear and doubt, suffered as a result of the sins of others (and sometimes their own), endured heartache and heartbreak, walked through loss and grief, and probably looked for the easy way out.

We need to remember these heroes of the faith *didn't know how their story would end*. And neither do we. That's why it's often so hard to believe God is working out everything in your life for your good and His glory—*we don't know the end of our story*. We doubt God's plan for us really is good. We aren't sure we can survive the storm we're in or if it's even worth it.

14

If there's only one thing you take away from this book, let it be this: God loves you. If you're feeling faithless, He will be faithful. You are not alone. The Bible encourages us to keep going and finish the race. How? By keeping our eyes on Jesus, "the author and finisher of our faith" (Heb. 12:2). Jesus is the *finisher* of our faith. Your story isn't finished yet. If we read those heroes' stories of faith in the Old Testament and stopped reading halfway through, we wouldn't get the whole picture. If we read the story of Shadrach, Meshach, and Abednego thrown into the fiery furnace for their faith and closed the book—we'd have missed the best part: God appeared in the fire and they came out unscathed!

He was with them the entire time, working it all together for their good and His glory! Your story isn't finished yet friend. God is for you! This is just the beginning.

"being confident of this very thing, that He who has begun a good work in you will complete it until the day of Jesus Christ." (Phil. 1:6)

CHAPTER 2

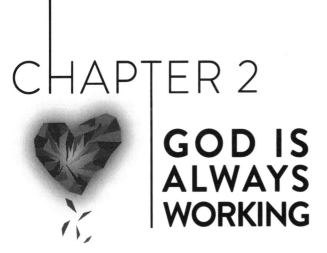

GOD IS ALWAYS WORKING

The story of Joseph is arguably one of the most well-known stories on suffering in the Bible. Joseph's story starts, as most do, long before his birth. His father Jacob, later renamed Israel by God, fell in love with a beautiful young woman named Rachel. Jacob loved Rachel so much that the seven years he worked for her father to marry her "seemed only a few days to him" (Gen. 29:20).

On the night of their wedding, Jacob entered his tent to meet his beloved bride, only to discover the next morning he'd been tricked: Rachel's father had sent her older sister, Leah, into the tent instead. Jacob was furious but agreed to work another seven years in exchange for his true love, Rachel. Can you imagine the rivalry between these two sisters, in-laws, daughters, and lovers? This was the family Joseph was born into.

Over the years Leah, though unloved, bore Jacob sons time and time again as Rachel looked on, unable to conceive. Finally, Rachel resolved to give her maid, Bilhah, to Jacob to bear children on her behalf. And Bilhah did bear children. But neither the rivalry nor the wounds ended there. Years went by, tears were shed, and bitter words exchanged, until one day the Bible says, "God remembered Rachel, and God listened to her and opened her womb" (Gen. 30:22). Rachel conceived and gave birth to a son named Joseph.

Some of you were born into families with existing rivalries and bitter feuds. You already know where this story is going. The battle didn't end with the long-awaited birth of Joseph to the barren-wife Rachel. It didn't end with the unloved-wife Leah bearing more children than her sister. The seeds of jealousy had been planted and sprouted up between the children of Rachel and Leah. The Bible picks up with Joseph's story in Genesis 37, detailing the favoritism his father showed him and the hatred his brothers felt because of it. His brothers grew tired of Joseph reporting on their bad behavior and their father's obvious affection for Joseph. And so, they devised a plan to kill him. At the last moment, however, they sold Joseph into slavery instead. It would be more than twenty years before they saw him again.

But God still had a plan for Joseph.

Joseph was seventeen years old when Midianite traders carted him off to Egypt, sold by his brothers for twenty pieces of silver. He was far from home. Alone. Afraid. And he was a slave. He had lost everything. Joseph spent the next thirteen years of his life in slavery working for a man named Potiphar, the captain of the Pharaoh's palace guard. At this point in Joseph's story, the author of the book of Genesis interrupts the narrative to make sure we're clear on something: "The Lord was with Joseph, and he was a successful man; and he was in the house of his master the Egyptian" (Gen. 39:2).

The Lord was *with* Joseph?!

Does this surprise you as it does me? Right in the middle of what seems like the worst time in Joseph's life, the Bible declares, "the Lord was with Joseph."

God still had a plan for Joseph.

A Biblical Perspective of Suffering

Jesus, speaking to His disciples said, "In the world you will have tribulation; but be of good cheer, I have overcome the world" (John 16:33b). You and I are going to suffer in this world. Pain and problems will follow us. Trials and troubles will be ours. Jesus doesn't qualify whether or not we deserve the trials and sorrows that come our way. He simply states they will come. Sometimes they come as a result of our own faults and failures. And sometimes, the faults and failures of others cost us deeply. But know this: the root of all suffering is sin and the effects of sin upon this world. The apostle Paul tells us "the wages of sin is death" (Rom. 6:23a).

All sin results in death in one form or another.

When we discuss suffering in light of what the Bible says about it, we must start with sin. And where did sin begin? The Garden of Eden. The Bible is very clear, God Himself does not tempt us to sin.

> "Let no one say when he is tempted, 'I am tempted by God'; for God cannot be tempted by evil, nor does He Himself tempt anyone. But each one is tempted when he is drawn away by his own desires and enticed. Then, when desire has conceived, it gives birth to sin; and sin, when it is full-grown, brings forth death." (James 1:13-15)

Paul explains a little bit more to us about how sin entered and corrupted the world in Romans 5. "Therefore, just as through one man sin entered the world, and death through sin, and thus death spread to all men, because all sinned" (Rom. 5:12). And yet, God doesn't leave us there. Paul goes on:

> "Nevertheless death reigned from Adam to Moses, even over those who had not sinned according to the likeness of the transgression of Adam, who is a type of Him who was to come. But the free gift is not like the offense. For if by

the one man's offense many died, much more the grace of God and the gift by the grace of the one Man, Jesus Christ, abounded to many." (Rom. 5:14-15)

Isn't that a relief?! Amen and thank You, God!

This is where our biblical perspective of suffering starts: God is not to blame for the sin and suffering in this world, man is. People are. We are. You may find yourself angry with God, or estranged from Him due to the trials you've suffered. This truth may be difficult for you to swallow right now. Anger is a normal response to pain and grief, and I don't judge you for it. God still loves you and desires a relationship with you. No matter what you're feeling right now, no matter what you've done or where you've been, whether you're the one who's caused the pain or you're a victim of the sins of others— God loves you. He has not forgotten about you. He still has a plan for you, to heal you, to comfort you.

The incredible promise we have, as those who love and follow God, is that God is still able to work together all these things—even the bad ones, the horrific ones, and the painful ones—for our good and His glory. For those of you who don't yet know God, who haven't yet called upon Jesus as your Lord and Savior—this world, with all of its pain and suffering, is the best it's ever going to get. That's it. But for those who love God, there is still something better, something more. Your suffering here is temporary. There is a day coming when there will be no more sorrows and no more tears. And even on this side of heaven, you can be sure the worst of your sufferings are being worked together into something good in Jesus.

But the Lord was with Joseph

Joseph spent years as a slave in Potiphar's house, and was eventually placed in charge of Potiphar's entire household. Potiphar trusted Joseph with everything he owned. At the end of those thirteen years, and just when you thought Joseph was a rags-to-riches story he was falsely accused of attempted rape by Potiphar's wife and thrown into prison. Again, the author of the book of Genesis interrupts the narrative to remind us that God was with Joseph.

> "**But the Lord was with Joseph** and showed him mercy, and He gave him favor in the sight of the keeper of the prison. And the keeper of the prison committed to Joseph's hand all the prisoners who were in the prison; whatever they did there, it was his doing. The keeper of the prison did not look into anything that was under Joseph's authority, because the Lord was with him; and whatever he did, the Lord made it prosper." (Gen. 39:21-23, emphasis added)

The second point in our biblical perspective of suffering is this: Your circumstances are not evidence of God's presence and goodness or lack thereof—God is good and He always and only does what is good. He is always with you. The Bible clearly states God was with Joseph and God loved Joseph. Nowhere does it mention Joseph had done something to displease God. Again, this may be challenging for you to process due to the hardships you've suffered. That doesn't make you a bad person, or a bad Christian by the way. It just means you're human. Like me, you have suffered through immense loss causing you to question if God is still good. *If God is good, if God really loves me, why would He allow this to happen in my life? Why would He allow such senseless pain and tragedy?* I've felt that way too. But we can trust Him in our pain. God is good and He always and only does what is good.

There are so many things we will never understand on this side of heaven. We just can't. God, speaking to the prophet Isaiah said, "'For My thoughts are not your thoughts, nor are your ways My ways,' says the Lord. 'For as the heavens are higher than the earth, so are My ways higher than your ways, and My thoughts than your thoughts'" (Isa. 55:8-9). There are things we won't understand here on earth, because we can't. We aren't God. His ways, His understanding, and His thoughts are too high for us to completely understand.

And friend—He isn't expecting you to understand. He's asking you to trust Him. To believe He is still good in spite of all that's happened to you. He knows you're struggling. The Bible says He's collected your tears in a bottle and has recorded each of your tears and sorrows in a book (Ps. 56:8). That's how special you are to Him.

God Intended It All for Good

Joseph's brothers did see him again more than twenty years after they sold him into slavery. Over twenty years after they dipped Joseph's beautiful robe in blood and led their father to believe he'd been attacked and eaten by a wild animal. Over twenty years of living with that lie. About twenty-two years after they'd sold Joseph, a severe famine entered the land. His brothers heard a rumor that Egypt still had grain. And it was true. Egypt had storehouses full of grain, while everywhere else the Bible says, "the famine was severe in all lands" (Gen. 41:57). The famine brought Joseph's brothers into Egypt face to face with Joseph.

Long gone were Joseph's days in prison. After accurately interpreting a dream of the Pharaoh's chief cupbearer and baker in prison, Joseph was called upon to interpret a dream for Pharaoh himself. God faithfully gave Joseph the interpretation for Pharaoh's dream as well: Seven years of great prosperity throughout Egypt followed by seven years of severe famine. After interpreting his dream, Joseph then gave Pharaoh suggestions on how to save the land of Egypt during the seven years of famine. Pharaoh liked the plan so much, he made Joseph second-in-command. He put Joseph in charge of an elaborate plan to collect deposits of grain from the people during the first seven years and redistribute the grain during the following seven years of famine.

Joseph was in charge when his brothers arrived in Egypt to buy grain.

God was with Joseph.

Joseph's brothers didn't recognize him, although Joseph immediately recognized them. And after a series of tests, Joseph revealed himself to his brothers. "'I am Joseph; does my father still live?' But his brothers could not answer him, for they were dismayed in his presence" (Gen. 45:3). Can you imagine it?! They were dismayed, stunned. But based on Joseph's response, we also surmise his brothers were afraid. "But now, do not therefore be grieved or angry with yourselves because you sold me here; for God sent me before you to preserve life" (Gen. 45:5). They had been found out, exposed.

And Joseph forgave them.

Now, for those of you who've read the story, I don't want you to skip over this next part. It's too important. This is not a rags-to-riches story, or a story on forgiveness. We can read the story of Joseph in a matter of minutes, but this was *decades of his life*. Joseph lived through slavery and imprisonment as a result of what his brothers did. He had good reason to be mad, or even bitter. But he forgave them and claimed that *God*, not his brothers, had sent him ahead to Egypt to preserve their lives. This wasn't a flash revelation for Joseph, a moment of profound forgiveness. This was a truth that had been growing in his heart for years: *God* had sent him ahead to Egypt. It was God's good plan laced with sorrow and suffering. Joseph was God's plan to save his family; his brothers who would later become the patriarchs of the twelve tribes of Israel. This was God's plan and Joseph accepted it.

What I want us to understand as we move forward is that God is good and yes, He is working all the time. Even in moments of tragedy and despair. Joseph's story was filled with suffering. Unjust treatment. Hardship. Perhaps yours is too? Joseph's understanding and acceptance of God's good plan didn't happen overnight. He likely spent years in Potiphar's house and prison wondering at the plan and goodness of God. I'm sure if someone had told him in prison, "Hey Joseph, God is going to work this together for your good!" he probably would have said, "That's great, but can you please get me out of prison NOW?!" Joseph had to work through these things with God just like you and I do.

Years later, Jacob, Joseph's father, died. He had lived long enough to see his beloved son Joseph again in Egypt and to move, along with his entire family, to join Joseph in Egypt. God really was working all things together for good. He had regained the son he thought had died and grandsons as well. After he passed, Joseph again addressed his brothers—now fearful that Joseph had just been pretending to forgive them for their father's sake. "'But as for you, you meant evil against me; but God meant it for good, in order to bring it about as it is this day, to save many people alive. Now therefore, do not be afraid; I will provide for you and your little ones.' And he comforted them and spoke kindly to them" (Gen. 50:20-21).

God intended it all for good. God was with Joseph all along. God was working even in that. And it's true for you too. Let this truth in Romans be a pillow that you rest your weary head on:

"And we know that all things work together for good to those who love God, to those who are the called according to His purpose." (Rom. 8:28)

CHAPTER 3

THE CRISIS IS GOD'S TOOL

In every great story the hero or heroine must overcome impossible odds—a painful loss, a debilitating fear, a physical limitation, a crisis of faith. These moments define us. They forever shape our future; the way we think about things, how we make decisions, why we do what we do. They are powerful, momentous, and rare. And more often than not, they come to us through the vehicle of pain.

In the book of 1 Samuel, we meet a woman named Hannah who is experiencing such a moment. Her introduction is simple: "And [Elkanah] had two wives: the name of one was Hannah, and the name of the other Peninnah. Peninnah had children, but Hannah had no children" (1 Sam. 1:2). Hannah was barren, unable to bear children. This, as many of you know very well, is a heavy burden to carry. Hannah was no different. She was suffering. Heartbroken. And she was alone. For although her husband Elkanah loved her, he did not share her sorrow. He didn't understand her loss, perhaps because he had children with another woman. And to make matters worse, the Bible says that Elkanah's other wife would mercilessly tease Hannah because of her barrenness.

"So it was, year by year, when she went up to the house of the Lord, that [Peninnah] provoked [Hannah]; therefore she wept and did not eat. Then Elkanah her husband said to her, 'Hannah, why do you weep? Why do you not eat? And why is your heart grieved? Am I not better to you than ten sons?'" (1 Sam. 1:7-8)

Hannah was in a desperate place. Her inability to have children affected her in every sense: physically, emotionally, socially, and spiritually. I won't even try to describe what it must have been like to be married to a man with another wife. To be married to a man who had children with another wife. To be married to a man who had children with another wife who taunted her. But for Hannah, this was also a cultural condition. She was shamed socially for inability to produce children. Children were seen as a blessing from God, and barrenness, an indication of sin, or worse, a curse from God.

We don't know what Hannah thought was the cause of her barrenness. Did she blame herself for some sin? Did she think God had forgotten her? Maybe she thought God had cursed her? The Bible doesn't tell us. We do know she's gone as far as she can go. She's reached a place of great anguish and bitterness of soul. She's been in the thick of an overwhelming and unrelenting trial for years. Hannah was in agony—misunderstood, tormented, mistreated, and desperate.

And in her pain, she goes to the Tabernacle of God.

The Battle

It's in times of great distress that God develops great faith. I'll not pretend the process is easy. When our son Eddie died in May of 2013, our lives became one desperate cry for God's presence. My family and I were broken—spiritually and emotionally. It was hard for us to see God during those dark days. We wanted to give up. It was a battle to press on and believe God was working all things together for our good and His glory. We were overwhelmed with grief and despair. Our relationship with God changed during that time. You may be surprised to hear our faith actually grew. I know I was. That crisis drew out of us a desperate plea for more of God's presence. *Don't give me something, God. Give me You!*

There is hope for you and me, just as there was for Hannah. But it's a struggle to get there.

The Bible teaches there is a battle going on all around us. As followers of Jesus Christ, the battle involves us too. It's not only all around us, it's raging within us as well. It's a battle of the flesh against the spirit. Paul wrote, "For the flesh lusts against the Spirit, and the Spirit against the flesh; and these are contrary to one another" (Gal. 5:17). When the Bible speaks of the flesh, it's not referring to the physical skin on your body. It's a technical word the Bible uses to describe life apart from God. It's the way we live life without God. For many of us, it's the way we lived life without God before we got saved. The flesh also refers to the sinful habit patterns we often revert to—even as Christians—when times get tough. The things we run to instead of God.

As we look at suffering in the Bible, we must remember that while God is not to blame for our sin and suffering, He does often use our pain for our good and His glory. There are times when God will allow our circumstances to bring us to point of complete desperation. A spiritual crisis hits us and we need to lay it all out on the table with God. It's a spiritual fork in the road, a place of great monumental decision. A place where we come to the end of ourselves and our resources. A place where all hope seems lost, but God. It's the moment when we stop running from God and start running to Him. The battle often presents you with a question: *Will you trust God?*

The crisis is your defining moment. Will you surrender your life to Him?

Nowhere to Go

As was their tradition each year, Hannah, Elkanah, Peninnah, and their children went to the Tabernacle for the annual time of worship and sacrifice. Following the sacrificial meal, Hannah went to the entrance of the Tabernacle and began to pray. The Bible says, "she was in bitterness of soul, and prayed to the Lord and wept in anguish" (1 Sam. 1:10). She did what many of us do when we don't know what else to do—she went to the church looking for help. Hannah had nowhere else to go. She had no one to turn to. She had exhausted her resources. Have you found yourself in a similar crisis of faith? Everything and everyone you've turned to has left you feeling alone, and even more empty than before.

> "Then she made a vow and said, 'O Lord of hosts, if You will indeed look on the affliction of Your maidservant and remember me, and not forget Your maidservant, but will give Your maidservant a male child, then I will give him to the Lord all the days of his life, and no razor shall come upon his head.'" (1 Sam. 1:11)

For Hannah, things are about to get worse. As she's pouring out her heart to the Lord, she's so overcome with grief and tears that although her lips are moving, no words are coming out. It was a deep groaning of her spirit calling out to God. It's a beautiful description of what Paul describes in Romans 8:26, "Likewise the Spirit also helps in our weaknesses. For we do not know what we should pray for as we ought, but the Spirit Himself makes intercession for us with groanings which cannot be uttered."

And as Hannah desperately, and tenderly pours out her heart to God, she is accused by Eli the priest of being drunk.

"Now Hannah spoke in her heart; only her lips moved, but her voice was not heard. Therefore Eli thought she was drunk. So Eli said to her, 'How long will you be drunk? Put your wine away from you!'" (1 Sam. 1:13-14)

Hannah needed compassion. She needed someone to serve her and lead her to the Lord. Instead, she was met with judgement and rejection. Sadly, many have had a similar experience in the church. They came in broken looking for grace and found judgement instead. It should not be so. I'm so sorry if this was your experience.

Hannah ministers to my heart because she didn't allow the failure of Eli the priest to become an excuse to not go to God. People will fail you. Pastors will fail you. Spouses will fail you. Friends will fail you. This world will fail you. You will be met by failure at every turn, but God will never fail you. Don't let people get in the way of finding and receiving comfort from the Divine Healer. In spite of all that Hannah had been through, including the rejection of Eli the priest, she pressed on to meet with the One who will never fail.

> "But Hannah answered and said, 'No, my lord, I am a woman of sorrowful spirit. I have drunk neither wine nor intoxicating drink, but have poured out my soul before the Lord . Do not consider your maidservant a wicked woman, for out of the abundance of my complaint and grief I have spoken until now.'" (1 Sam. 1:15-16)

Seek First the Kingdom

When Eli heard Hannah's answer, he responded, "'Go in peace, and the God of Israel grant your petition which you have asked of Him'" (1 Sam. 1:17). And Hannah believed him. The Bible says, "So the woman went her way and ate, and her face was no longer sad" (1 Sam. 1:18b). This amazes me, because nothing about Hannah's situation had changed. As far as we know, and as far as she knows, she's still barren. Her husband is still married to another woman who ridiculed her. She's still an outcast of society. The only thing changed is Hannah's heart, or you might say, the attitude of her heart. She believed God would grant her request. She trusted God.

You can trust God, too.

Hannah's desperation drove her to a place of deep trust and surrender to God. This is what God wants for you and me. It's also what He wants from you and me. Jesus said, "'But seek first the kingdom of God and His righteousness, and all these things shall be added to you'" (Matt. 6:33). God's desire is that our hearts would respond and resonate with the words of Jesus, saying, *Yes, Lord! I want to seek the things of the kingdom! I trust You will take care of me!*

God doesn't want to take from you. He wants more of you, so He can add more to you.

The Bible is full of ordinary men and women demonstrating extraordinary faith. Their stories encourage and inspire us but we must not forget *they were real people just like you and me.* I'm sure Hannah battled to get to the temple that day. Maybe she didn't want to go. She probably struggled to lay her burden down at the altar and fought to walk away in faith—believing God had heard her prayer.

I'm reminded of Abraham, another man of great faith, who also battled to get there. His wife Sarah was barren. When Abraham was one hundred years old, Sarah was ninety, God promised them a son—a miracle of the womb they named Isaac. Years later, in the biggest crisis of Abraham's life, God said to Abraham, "'Take now your son, your only son Isaac, whom you love, and go to the land of Moriah, and offer him there as a burnt offering on one of the mountains of which I shall tell you'" (Gen. 22:2). Perhaps you've heard the story. Abraham did what God asked and took his son up the mountain fully intending to sacrifice what God had promised him—his most treasured possession—his son, Isaac.

Like Hannah, Abraham trusted God.

We learn from the book of Hebrews Abraham believed "that God was able to raise him up, even from the dead" (Heb. 11:19). God intervened up on Mount Moriah and stopped Abraham from killing his son. Because God wasn't really asking Abraham for Isaac. He was asking for Abraham. Do you trust Me Abraham? *Will you surrender even your most treasured possession to Me?*

God's Answer

Not too long after, Elkanah, his wives Hannah and Peninnah, and their children returned home from worshipping the Lord to their home in Ramah. "And Elkanah knew Hannah his wife, and the Lord remembered her. So it came to pass in the process of time that Hannah conceived and bore a son, and called his name Samuel, saying, 'Because I have asked for him from the Lord'" (1 Sam. 1:19b-20).

God granted Hannah's request. You might be tempted to think, *Well, Hannah got what she wanted. I didn't.* Or, *If I knew I was going to get what I've asked God for, I would trust Him too!* But this story isn't about asking and receiving. It's a story about trust and surrender.

Hannah trusted God. Her life changed that heartbreaking day at the Tabernacle, much like Abraham's life changed at the top of Mount Moriah. All she wanted was a son, and all God wanted was more of her. Total devotion to the eternal things of God. The crisis was God's tool to get more of her.

> "Now when she had weaned him, she took him up with her, with three bulls, one ephah of flour, and a skin of wine, and brought him to the house of the Lord in Shiloh. And the child was young. Then they slaughtered a bull, and brought the child to Eli. And she said, 'O my lord! As your soul lives, my lord, I am the woman who stood by you here, praying to the Lord . For this child I prayed, and the Lord has granted me my petition which I asked of Him. Therefore I also have lent him to the Lord ; as long as he lives he shall be lent to the Lord.' So they worshiped the Lord there." (1 Sam. 1: 24-28)

There are moments that forever shape our future. The question is, *what will we do with them?* For Hannah and for Abraham, their crisis led them to a place of worship. Times of severe spiritual crisis have a way of doing that, don't they? What starts out as a battle to run to God, to draw close to Him, becomes deep times of prayer with God. We wrestle in the spiritual realm, trying to make sense of what we know to be true of God and of our own brokenness. These times of prayer almost always end in worship. Like Hannah, like Abraham—our faith grows. We come into a deeper relationship with God. It's in times of great difficulty that God develops great prayer lives. God wants to deepen your relationship with Him too.

Years after Hannah and Abraham received their answer, their gift from God; and years after Hannah and Abraham offered their lives to God; there would be another gift given from God. God would send His only Son, the Lamb of God. "For God so loved the world that He gave His only begotten Son, that whoever believes in Him should not perish but have everlasting life" (John 3:16). God the Father, in the ultimate act of love and mercy sent His only Son, born to die, as the payment for our sins. God wasn't taking from us, He was adding to us by providing the answer to our most desperate cry, the answer to our groaning spirits.

God's answer is more of His Presence and more of His Son—the remedy for sin.

Only in Jesus do we have the promise that God is working all of these things together for our good and His glory. Only in the Father do we have the answer to our desperate heart's cry. Who can save us from this misery? God has provided Himself, a Savior—Christ Jesus.

This is your defining moment, friend. Let's not waste it. Your crisis has a purpose. Will you trust God? Will you surrender your life, your will to Him?

"But when the kindness and the love of God our Savior toward man appeared, not by works of righteousness which we have done, but according to His mercy He saved us, through the washing of regeneration and renewing of the Holy Spirit" (Titus 3:4-5)

CHAPTER 4

JESUS IS THE FOUNDATION

In Matthew 7:24-27, Jesus gave an illustration to the large crowd gathered around him. Two people built a house. The first person built their house on a solid rock. The second person built their house on sand. The difference in the two homes was only in their foundation, but neither knew the dissimilarity until a storm came. And a mighty storm did come. The rain pounded down on both of those homes, the river flooded, and a tornado hit, but nothing moved the house built on the solid rock. The house on the sand didn't fare as well. When the storm came, it collapsed upon itself as the sand was washed away.

The storm revealed the foundation the homes were built upon. And in life, storms will reveal the foundation your life is built on as well.

There will be trials, there will be storms, and there will be suffering in this life. You may be in the midst of a trial as you read this. You may have been in a season of suffering for years. There's no end in sight. You aren't sure if you can keep going. God hasn't forgotten you, in fact, He wants to give you the strength to bear up spiritually under these heavy earthly burdens. He wants to restore the hope for a future you can only find in Him. He is able to use these storms, yes, even these horrible events, and work them together for your good and His glory. He really can. But in order to withstand the storms, our foundation must be built upon Jesus. He is the Solid Rock that the first home was built upon. "This is the 'stone which was rejected by you builders, which has become the chief cornerstone'" (Acts 4:11).

It's time to start building on the foundation of Jesus Christ.

The Greatest Witness

Hebrews 12:1 says, "Therefore we also, since we are surrounded by so great a cloud of witnesses, let us lay aside every weight, and the sin which so easily ensnares us, and let us run with endurance the race that is set before us." Joseph, Hannah, Abraham, and all the heroes in the Hall of Faith are witnesses to the life of faith. Their lives testify that God is good and He works all things together for our good. And now they surround us, witnesses to our lives of faith, which also testify that God is good, and He really is working all things together for our good. But the ultimate revelation of God's goodness, the best example of God working for our good, and the greatest witness to the life of faith, is Jesus.

Speaking of Jesus, John wrote, "In the beginning was the Word, and the Word was with God, and the Word was God. He was in the beginning with God. All things were made through Him, and without Him nothing was made that was made" (John 1:1-3). Jesus, the Word of God, became the "Lamb of God" (John 1:36) who takes away the sin of the world! The book of Romans puts it this way:

> "For what the law could not do in that it was weak through the flesh, God did by sending His own Son in the likeness of sinful flesh, on account of sin: He condemned sin in the flesh, that the righteous requirement of the law might be fulfilled in us who do not walk according to the flesh but according to the Spirit." (Rom. 8:3-4)

Jesus died so we could live. Jesus lived so we could live more abundantly. "For He made Him who knew no sin to be sin for us, that we might become the righteousness of God in Him" (2 Cor. 5:21).

Jesus was tempted in the same way we are; He was exposed to the same fallen world we are; and He was limited by His humanity just as we are. He suffered just as we all do. He shared in our humanity, and yet, He did not sin. The book of Hebrews says, "in all things He had to be made like His brethren, that He might be a merciful and faithful High Priest in things pertaining to God, to make propitiation for the sins of the people. For in that He Himself has suffered, being tempted, He is able to aid those who are tempted" (Heb. 2:17-18).

Jesus lived a perfect life of faith. And even Jesus suffered.

Looking to Jesus

The writer of the book of Hebrews encourages us to run the race God has set before us with "endurance" (Heb. 12:1). The word used for endurance in the original Greek is *hypomonē*. It means "a patient, steadfast waiting for." It's made up of two root words; *hypo*, meaning, "under," and *menō*, meaning "to remain, abide." It carries the idea of bearing up under pressure and not giving up. Of steadying on, not quitting, and not turning back. As you and I both know, there are some trials where this feels downright impossible. *Run? With endurance? I can't even get out of bed right now!* And friend, I've been there. You feel like you want to give up, or you shouldn't have to suffer as much as you are. But let me encourage you in this—if Jesus, the Son of God, also suffered in this life and He is the greatest witness of a life of faith, then so will you. There are times when it feels impossible, which is why the author of Hebrews goes on to explain how we do it: "looking unto Jesus, the author and finisher of our faith" (Heb. 12:2a). The only way forward is by *keeping our eyes on Jesus. By looking to Jesus.* When we keep our eyes on Jesus it gives us the perspective we need to endure.

What did Jesus suffer? What did He endure? In His short thirty-three years on this earth, He was ridiculed, rejected, despised, mocked, fatigued, ignored, condemned, wrongfully accused, doubted, insulted, beaten, whipped, scourged, betrayed by His own disciple, denied by His best friend, and given a criminal's death upon a cross. He was let down by His closest friends when He asked them to pray and keep watch in His hour of deepest need. He was abandoned by everyone—including His heavenly Father, for a moment. And that's just a very small snapshot of the earthly reward Jesus received after thirty-three years of perfect living.

William Barkley, in his commentary on the Gospel of Matthew writes:

> "Roman scourging was a terrible torture. The victim was stripped. His hands were tied behind him, and he was tied to a post with his back bent double and conveniently exposed to the lash. The lash itself was a long, leather thong, studded at intervals with sharpened pieces of bone and pellets of lead. Such scourging always preceded crucifixion, and it reduced the naked body to strips of raw flesh and inflamed and bleeding wounds. Men died under it, and most men lost their reason under it, and few remained conscious to the end of it."[4]

You may feel no one understands you, no one has endured the kind of torment and torture you have—physically, emotionally, mentally, or spiritually. Even people who have been through similar struggles don't understand you. And you'd be correct. You will not find the comfort you're looking for here on earth. No one here will ever fully understand what you've gone through, or what you're going through. King Solomon couldn't find any comfort or satisfaction in this world and he had everything this world has to offer. But Jesus knows. He understands what you're going through, not only because He created you and knows you better than you know yourself, but because *He also suffered in the same ways we do.* He willingly lived this life in human form, filled with suffering, for you.

"Seeing then that we have a great High Priest who has passed through the heavens, Jesus the Son of God, let us hold fast our confession. For we do not have a High Priest who cannot sympathize with our weaknesses, but was in all points tempted as we are, yet without sin. Let us therefore come boldly to the throne of grace, that we may obtain mercy and find grace to help in time of need." (Heb. 4:14-16)

Fellowship in Suffering

Because Jesus suffered, we will also suffer. We bear the death of Jesus in our earthly bodies, patiently enduring the effects of sin on this world, so that we can also share in the life Jesus came to offer us in our spiritual bodies. We were made for more than this. And in Jesus, we have more than this life will ever be able to offer. This is the incredible truth for those of us who have been born again as followers of Jesus Christ: When you gave your life to Jesus, you were spiritually born again. Sin, death, and the grave no longer have any hold over you. You are a new creation. And as a new creation in Christ Jesus, you now get to share in His victory. "The sting of death is sin, and the strength of sin is the law. But thanks be to God, who gives us the victory through our Lord Jesus Christ" (1 Cor. 15:56-57).

Here's how Paul puts it in the book of Romans, "For if by the one man's offense death reigned through the one, much more those who receive abundance of grace and of the gift of righteousness will reign in life through the One, Jesus Christ" (Rom. 5:17).

The truth is—we will experience suffering whether we proclaim Jesus as our Savior or not. That's a given. None of us will escape it. But as believers, we have been given victory over sin. Remember, sin is the root cause of all suffering. It's the reason the world is the way it is. As you and I both know, the effects of sin upon this world are devastating. We see it daily in our physical bodies as they age and grow weak, and we see it in the tragedies happening all over the world. The consequences of sin are horrific. As believers, we still experience the effects of sin upon this world and in our lives, but we have victory over sin and death and the promise of redemption through Jesus Christ.

What does this mean for those of us who love Jesus? It means that the effects of sin hold no power over us. It means that God is able to redeem the bad things, the horrible things, the tragic things and work them together for good through the death and resurrection of Jesus. Jesus defeated our worst enemy on the cross—sin and death. That's our worst enemy! Jesus, through His resurrection, defeated both sin and death on your behalf. We fellowship with Him in His suffering and we also share with Him in His victory.

God really is working all things together for our good and His glory.

Paul, writing to the Corinthian church described our suffering this way: "For our light affliction, which is but for a moment, is working for us a far more exceeding and eternal weight of glory, while we do not look at the things which are seen, but at the things which are not seen. For the things which are seen are temporary, but the things which are not seen are eternal" (2 Cor. 4:17-18).

Our afflictions are working for us, not against us. My friend, Pastor David Guzik, writes in his Bible Commentary on this passage:

> "Yes, our affliction is light. Our affliction is light compared to what others are suffering. Our affliction is light compared to what we deserve. Our affliction is light compared to what Jesus suffered for us. Our affliction is light compared to the blessings we enjoy. Our affliction is light as we experience the sustaining power of God's grace. Our

affliction is light when we see the glory that it's leading to. And we can really say, with Paul, 'our light affliction.'"[5]

Building on the Right Foundation

The way we build or rebuild our lives upon the foundation of Jesus Christ is by "looking unto Jesus" (Heb. 12:2a). Jesus said, "'If anyone desires to come after Me, let him deny himself, and take up his cross, and follow Me'" (Matt. 16:24). The life and death of Jesus is our foundation. We build our foundation upon Jesus by giving up our old way of living life, picking up our cross—the sufferings we endure as believers—and following Him. We build on the foundation of Jesus by looking unto Him. The author of the book of Hebrews goes on to say, "let us run with endurance the race that is set before us, looking unto Jesus, the author and finisher of our faith, who **for the joy that was set before Him endured the cross, despising the shame, and has sat down at the right hand of the throne of God"** (Heb. 12:1b-2, emphasis added).

Jesus endured the cross, disregarding its shame, because of the joy awaiting Him. Friend, that joy was you. That joy was me. Jesus was willing to endure the suffering and run the race God set before Him because of the joy awaiting Him at the end. It was worth it for Him. And it will be worth it for you too. I know you probably don't feel that way right now. You just want your trial to be over. Maybe you want the entire race to be done. But believe me, it will be worth it. Paul said, "For I consider that the sufferings of this present time are not worthy to be compared with the glory which shall be revealed in us" (Rom. 8:18). The sufferings we experience now cannot even be compared with the future glory. The difference is so vast, so incomparable, your current suffering equals out to nothing when placed on the same scale with the glory that is coming. Our sufferings here on earth aren't easy. At times, they feel downright unbearable. But they are not to be compared to glory that awaits us.

It may be you've found yourself in a place of rebuilding. You've survived the worst of the storm, but you've realized your home was built on sand. Maybe you didn't realize what you were doing or you thought you could get away with it. But now, as you look around at the shambles, you get it. Your foundation wasn't as strong as you thought it was. If your foundation is built upon anything other than Jesus, it won't last. It's sand. It's here today and gone tomorrow. Trials and suffering will expose the foundation of your life every time.

Jesus said, "whoever hears these sayings of Mine, and does them, I will liken him to a wise man who built his house on the rock" (Matt. 7:24). It's time to start rebuilding on Jesus. It's not going to be easy, but God will help you. Your Champion, Jesus, has gone before you. You only need to look to Him.

> "We are hard-pressed on every side, yet not crushed; we are perplexed, but not in despair; persecuted, but not forsaken; struck down, but not destroyed—always carrying about in the body the dying of the Lord Jesus, that the life of Jesus also may be manifested in our body." (2 Cor. 4:8-10)

CHAPTER 5

COUNT IT ALL JOY

In 2 Kings 6, Elisha the prophet and his servant awoke to find themselves surrounded by a vast army. The king of Aram was at war with the nation of Israel. Time and time again he sent his troops out to attack Israel, and each time they were defeated. The king of Aram couldn't believe it. Not only were his troops unsuccessful, it was as if the Israelites knew he was going to attack.

> "He called his servants and said to them, 'Will you not show me which of us is for the king of Israel?' And one of his servants said, 'None, my lord, O king; but Elisha, the prophet who is in Israel, tells the king of Israel the words that you speak in your bedroom.'" (2 Kings 6:11b-12)

Infuriated, the king sent his troops complete with chariots and horses to seize two men—Elisha and his servant. Early the next morning, Elisha's servant saw the troops, horses, and chariots. They were surrounded. He was expecting just another day when suddenly, the bottom fell out. He was petrified. I know exactly what Elisha's servant experienced that morning. You too? You've lived through the nightmare of going to bed thinking everything was okay only to discover the next morning it would never be the same again. You know what it feels like to have your heart fall through your chest down into your stomach.

"'Do not fear, for those who are with us are more than those who are with them.' And Elisha prayed, and said, 'Lord, I pray, open his eyes that he may see.' Then the Lord opened the eyes of the young man, and he saw. And behold, the mountain was full of horses and chariots of fire all around Elisha." (2 Kings 6:16-17)

Elisha and his servant both saw the Aramean troops. They both saw the chariots and the horses. They were both surrounded. The only difference was their perspective—and that perspective directed their response. The servant saw only what was happening in the earthly realm. Elisha saw the Aramean troops, but he also saw what was happening in the spiritual realm. There was an even greater army—angels and chariots of fire—surrounding the Aramean army.

A New Perspective

Our perspective, whether earthly or spiritual, informs our response. That's why it's imperative before we move on, to ask God to open our eyes and our minds to have the right perspective, the spiritual perspective of what's happening in our own lives, in the lives of our loved ones, and in our world right now. The perspective with which you look at the world will dramatically affect how you choose to move forward—in this book and in life. We need to have eyes to see what God is doing in the spiritual realm.

Another way of talking about your spiritual perspective might be to say, looking at your situation through eyes of faith. The Bible says, "Now faith is the substance of things hoped for, the evidence of things not seen" (Heb. 11:1). Faith is the means by which we connect to the spiritual realm. It's the belief that God exists, and that He is who He says He is. So when we talk about having a spiritual perspective like Elisha, I'm suggesting we choose to believe what the Bible says about life, death, heaven, hell, and suffering is all true.

I'm suggesting that although we cannot see the spiritual realm with our physical eyes, we open our spiritual eyes, our eyes of faith, to see what God is doing.

Here are some of the biblical truths we've learned so far that may help you adjust your spiritual lenses:

Everyone suffers. You are not alone.

God loves you. He has a good plan for you and your life.

God is not to blame for our suffering. Suffering comes from sin.

God is working all things together for your good and His glory.

God will use anything—even your pain—to draw you closer to Himself.

I think it's important to note your perspective doesn't change your situation. Both Elisha and his servant were still surrounded by the Aramean army. Their circumstances hadn't changed. Your new perspective will not necessarily change your situation, but it will radically impact how you move forward in it. The psalmist wrote, "Many are the afflictions of the righteous, But the Lord delivers him out of them all" (Pss. 34:19). An earthly perspective leads to fear, much like Elisha's servant, while a spiritual perspective invites us to hope. The right perspective can restore your confidence and give you the endurance you need to make it through another day.

Now, I realize you may be thinking, *Another day? I need the strength to get through another hour.* With the right perspective, and the power of God, you can get through another hour. Pretty soon, hours will become days, days will become weeks, and weeks will become months. Before you know it, you'll find the presence and power of God is a great comfort in your time of need.

Letters from Prison

Much of what we now know as the New Testament of the Bible was written by a man named Paul. Prior to becoming a Christian, he was known as Saul of Tarsus, a Jewish zealot and Pharisee (religious and governmental leaders of the Jewish community). Acts 9 tells the story of Paul's conversion. After threatening to kill all Christians, he traveled to Damascus with letters from the high priest authorizing him to arrest any followers of Jesus he might find at the local synagogues. On the way, a light from heaven shone around him. Saul fell to the ground, and heard a voice speaking to him.

"'Saul, Saul, why are you persecuting Me?'

And he said, 'Who are You, Lord?'

Then the Lord said, 'I am Jesus, whom you are persecuting. It is hard for you to kick against the goads.'

So he, trembling and astonished, said, 'Lord, what do You want me to do?'

Then the Lord said to him, 'Arise and go into the city, and you will be told what you must do.'" (Acts 9:4-6)

Paul became a follower of Jesus that day. He would later go on to write thirteen of the twenty-seven books in the New Testament of the Bible.

And he suffered greatly.

Speaking of his tribulations, Paul wrote:

"From the Jews five times I received forty stripes minus one. Three times I was beaten with rods; once I was stoned; three times I was shipwrecked; a night and a day I have been in the deep; in journeys often, in perils of waters, in perils of robbers, in perils of my own countrymen, in perils of the Gentiles, in perils in the city, in perils in the wilderness, in perils in the sea, in perils among false brethren; in weariness and toil, in sleeplessness often, in hunger and thirst, in fastings often, in cold and nakedness." (2 Cor. 11:24-27)

Paul wrote the books of Ephesians, Philippians, Colossians, and Philemon from prison. He was in chains, and yet able to say, "and if I am being poured out as a drink offering on the sacrifice and service of your faith, I am glad and rejoice with you all" (Phil. 2:17). Later, Paul wrote, "I suffer trouble as an evildoer, even to the point of chains; but the word of God is not chained. Therefore I endure all things for the sake of the elect, that they also may obtain the salvation which is in Christ Jesus with eternal glory" (2 Tim. 2:9-10).

Paul saw the chains and the prison walls. But he also saw the hand of God at work in his life. His response was joy. Peter also encourages us to rejoice in the middle of our trials:

"Beloved, do not think it strange concerning the fiery trial which is to try you, as though some strange thing happened to you; **but rejoice** to the extent that you partake of Christ's sufferings, that when His glory is revealed, you may also be glad with exceeding joy." (1 Pet. 4:12-13, emphasis added)

Rejoice?

This is the response to the new perspective God is working out in you—*Rejoice!* Don't misunderstand what Peter is saying here. He's not saying rejoice for the trials, *Whoa, this is so good, God! Give me more trials! Oh, I'm so happy. Give me more! Give it to my friends, and my neighbors, too!* That's not wise. But rather, we're taught to rejoice in the trials— while we're going through them. James, the brother of Jesus, put it this way, "count it all joy when you fall into various trials" (James 1:2). The New Living Translation rewords James 1:2 as, "consider it

47

an opportunity for great joy." *Count it all joy? Consider it an opportunity for great joy?!* It's a mindset shift, a change in perspective, which alters our natural response. Peter and James are inviting you to adjust your lenses to see into the spiritual realm, not simply look at what you see happening in the earthly realm.

Perspective changes everything. It enables us and empowers us to say in times of trouble, "the joy of the Lord is [my] strength!" (Neh. 8:10)

Count It All Joy

One of the last letters Paul wrote is now known as the book of 2 Timothy. It was a letter to Timothy, his son in the faith, written from his prison cell. Paul knew the end of his life was near. He was alone, and cold. It was likely very damp in his cell. He reminds Timothy, "Bring the cloak that I left with Carpus at Troas when you come—and the books, especially the parchments" (2 Tim. 4:13). These aren't exactly the conditions we'd expect for a brother in the Lord who gave so much of his life for others, who suffered so much. As someone who was near the end of his trials on this earth, Paul wrote: "But you be watchful in all things, endure afflictions, do the work of an evangelist, fulfill your ministry" (2 Tim. 4:5).

Paul experienced more suffering than most of us will encounter in our lifetime.

"Blessed be the God and Father of our Lord Jesus Christ, the Father of mercies and God of all comfort, who comforts us in all our tribulation, that we may be able to comfort those who are in any trouble, with the comfort with which we ourselves are comforted by God. For as the sufferings of Christ abound in us, so our consolation also abounds through Christ." (2 Cor. 1:3-5)

Paul knew what it meant to suffer. And he knew what it meant to receive God's comfort.

Perhaps you have been through so much pain and suffering your heart has grown calloused. Your pain is so hard and so deep you're resistant to receive. I understand, and I don't stand in judgement upon you. Too many people have tried to tell you they understand when they really don't. Too many people have tried to place a scripture Band-Aid over your pain, and it's hurt you. Paul said he suffered *to comfort you*. He has the authority to speak into your pain, because he really has suffered.

> "Now if we are afflicted, it is for your consolation and salvation, which is effective for enduring the same sufferings which we also suffer. Or if we are comforted, it is for your consolation and salvation. And our hope for you is steadfast, because we know that as you are partakers of the sufferings, so also you will partake of the consolation." (2 Cor. 1:6-7)

I've met many believers over the years who have tried to put a good face on suffering. They tried to smile through it, thinking it was what God called them to do. If you asked how they're doing, they'd grin and say, "I'm blessed." But that isn't the whole truth. They are blessed, that's true. They've been forgiven and set free from the power of sin in their lives! But they are also hurting. Has that been your story? Perhaps you've been too afraid to say how you're really doing, worried you'll sound ungrateful, or you'll be judged for your pain? Paul and others also experienced many trials, much difficulty, and tremendous pain. The key that unlocked their ability to rejoice in the midst of their suffering was their perspective.

In the book of Romans, Paul wrote, "And not only that, but we also glory in tribulations, knowing that tribulation produces perseverance" (Rom. 5:3). He went on to say, "For I consider that the sufferings of this present time are not worthy to be compared with the glory which shall be revealed in us" (Rom. 8:18). The word that Paul used for *consider*, means "to reckon, count, compute, calculate, count over."[6] Paul thought about his suffering. He considered it. He took it into account—the beatings, the stoning when he nearly died, the shipwrecks—and he reckoned his sufferings were not worthy to be compared with the coming glory.

Here's my paraphrase of what Paul is saying, "Listen, guys, I don't consider the sufferings of this present time to be compared to what's up ahead, of what God has waiting for us, of the joy that's going to be when we meet Jesus face-to-face, of the fulness of love you're going to experience. It doesn't compare."

Friend, we will be able to count it all joy, to rejoice, to consider our sufferings not worthy to be compared to the coming glory when we choose to see the world through spiritual eyes of faith. When we understand there is another reality, wherein God is working out our trials for our good and His glory and using them to draw us closer to Himself. Whatever you're going through right now—as heavy as it is, as horrific and painful as it is—is not worthy to be compared with the glory coming for you.

"My brethren, count it all joy when you fall into various trials, knowing that the testing of your faith produces patience." (James 1:2-3)

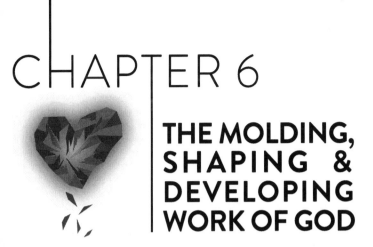

CHAPTER 6

THE MOLDING, SHAPING & DEVELOPING WORK OF GOD

As we continue through our biblical perspective of suffering, I realize you may not yet be ready to move forward. When Paul said, "count it all joy" (James 1:2), you just couldn't do it. I've been there. Some days, I'm not ready to count it all joy either. I understand this is God's will for my life, but my heart says, "No, thank you." I'm still working through these truths myself. Not everything that happens is good. We're all going through something. But God's promise to you is that He is able to work it all together for your good and His glory. We can be encouraged in that.

The Potter's House

The prophet Jeremiah lived during a very dark time in the nation of Israel's history. The country was steeped in idolatry. No one was listening to or even looking for God. God called Jeremiah to give them a message—one that Jeremiah repeated again and again as he wept over their idolatry and departure from worshiping the Lord. We often call Jeremiah the Weeping Prophet, because no one we're aware of responded to his forty plus years of ministry. He had a particularly difficult job. One day however, Jeremiah received a word from the Lord for himself.

"The word which came to Jeremiah from the Lord, saying: 'Arise and go down to the potter's house, and there I will cause you to hear My words.' Then I went down to the potter's house, and there he was, making something at the wheel. And the vessel that he made of clay was marred . . . " (Jer. 18:1-4)

God called Jeremiah to visit the potter's house. While there, Jeremiah watched as the potter worked with a vessel on his wheel. It was an illustration meant to encourage Jeremiah, as well as you and me. In this illustration, the potter is our loving Father in heaven and we are the clay. Yes, we are the lump of clay on the potter's wheel. The spinning wheel is life and the experiences of life. As Jeremiah continued to watch the potter molding and shaping, he noticed something—the vessel was marred. The word marred in the Hebrew is *shachath*, meaning "ruined."[7] Good for nothing. Broken. The lump of clay had been corrupted somehow.

I originally shared only the first part of verse 4 with you, because that's where a lot of people stop. They feel like the marred vessel on the potter's wheel. They believe they are ruined beyond repair. There's no help for them. They see the ruined clay, they see their own broken life, and they stop. It feels like everything the Potter did was a waste. They believe their life is over. But everything isn't over for the marred vessel in the illustration. Let's look at verse 4 in its entirety:

"And the vessel that he made of clay was marred **in the hand of the potter**; so he made it again into another vessel, as it seemed good to the potter to make" (Jer. 18:4, emphasis added).

Years ago, I spoke with an incredible potter who shared a remarkable bit of insight with me about this passage: *The potter already knows what the clay will be before he places it on the wheel.* Is the Potter, our Loving Father, surprised when things go wrong or when it looks like we need to start all over again? Are we ever really ruined in the

Potter's hand? Is there anything outside of God's ability to repair, rebuild, and restore? The answer my friend, is no. There is nothing so corrupted that God cannot repair. There is no life so destroyed that God cannot rebuild. There is no person so lost that God cannot restore. There is hope.

You are safe in the Potter's hands.

Rejoicing in the Pressing

In the book of Romans, Paul explains further why we rejoice even during suffering. We rejoice because our hardships aren't worthy to be compared to the coming glory—yes—and we also rejoice because these trials *are working for us right now.* "And not only that, but we also glory in tribulations, knowing that tribulation produces perseverance; and perseverance, character; and character, hope" (Rom. 5:3-4). Your current sufferings, your trials, your struggles *are working for you.* They are producing something for you in the spiritual realm, the benefits of which, you get to enjoy in the here and now.

If you travel to Israel today, you can still see replicas of the ancient olive press, used to create oil. The press consists of a giant basin, with a large stone that rolls around within a groove inside the basin. When harvested, the olives are too hard to be pressed. Instead, they are crushed in the basin by the rolling stone, pits and all. The crushing continues, round and round, until the olives are so finely ground, they become a paste. The word Paul used for *tribulations* in Romans 5:3-4 means, "a pressing, pressure" or crushing.[8] It's the picture of the ancient olive press. In essence, Paul is saying, "We can rejoice when we find ourselves in the olive press, in the crushing. We can rejoice when our life, our lump of clay, is suddenly pressed down and reshaped in the Potter's hands because we know there is an intended purpose" (Rom. 5:3-4, Jer. 18:1-4, my paraphrase).

Why would being compared to the crushing of olives or the molding of clay cause us to rejoice? It's our biblical perspective of suffering that helps us understand we rejoice not for the trials themselves, but for the work the Father is doing in our lives. Let me remind you, before you became a believer, the suffering in this world was just that—suffering. We had no promise of a better future. We had no promise that it would all work out. But in Christ, we have the promise of eternal life, and also the promise that even our suffering is working for our good and God's glory.

And not only that, but now "we have peace with God through our Lord Jesus Christ" (Rom. 5:1). Whether we walk with God or not, we will experience pain in this life. The hope for the believer is this: Your relationship both to and in Christ—unmerited, undeserved, unearned privilege—means even these afflictions are not outside of His ability to transform and redeem in your life. He has redeemed us in death, and He is redeeming us in life. The painful results of sin are being redeemed into something good for us.

And in that, we can rejoice.

The Molding, Shaping, and Developing

There is the temptation, when we see those around us going through trials, to think, *I could never survive what they went through* or, *They're much stronger than I am—I could never do that.* This is a serious error. Had you asked them prior to the trial, I'm sure they'd have said the same thing of themselves, *I could never do that.* God provided what they needed to patiently endure their trial as they experienced it. Do you remember manna, the food from heaven God provided the children of Israel as they journeyed through the wilderness? Each day, they awoke to find the ground covered with manna, and each day they collected enough manna *for the day.* God's provision for us, in good times and bad, is always perfect. It's always just what we need. His grace comes pouring in the moment we need it most.

Our trials are opportunities for the Potter to work in our lives. If given the choice, none of us would choose suffering. None of us are better at it or more naturally more equipped to suffer than others. If we can work, wiggle, or manipulate our way out of it—we will. We don't want any part of it! We avoid it at all costs. But suffering is often the vehicle that causes us to yield to the Father's loving hands. It drives us to cry out, "There's nothing I can do! God help me!" Trials will bring us to our knees. They are the crushing of the olive press and the pressing of the Potter's hands molding and shaping us into the image of Christ.

Your trials are producing in you perseverance, strength of character, and hope.

It's interesting to me that the Greek word used for perseverance or endurance in Romans 5:3-4, *hypomenō*, is similar to a word we've come across before hypomonē. Both words can be translated as endurance, but in *hypomenō* there's the additional idea of enduring bravely and calmly even under great trials.[9] It's a picture of a tree standing strong at the top of a hill. The storms come and although the tree bends and bows, it does not topple over. When the storm passes, the tree remains standing. It's normal for us to want to throw in the towel while surrounded by storms, to topple over under pressure. And yet, the Potter's hands have built into us the ability to not quit. To stand strong. Although we are pressed down and the molding is uncomfortable, we are safe in the Potter's hands. He is not taking from us. He is adding to us hypomenō—through trials— as He carefully molds and shapes our lives.

Notice, the endurance is built into the tree, into us, through storms. Each time the tree bends low under the wind, its roots grow stronger and deeper, making the tree more able to withstand the next storm. This endurance in our lives, this ability to stand strong even though storms threaten to uproot us, produces character. The

King James Version translates this as "experience" (Rom. 5:4, KJV). As the Potter molds and shapes your life through trials, He builds into you character, proven experience—making you more and more like Jesus.

When you think about the people you've turned to in the midst of hard times, who are they? They are people you trust, and no doubt, people who have been through hard times themselves. We don't turn to people who've never experienced hard times, or act as though life is always great for them, do we? Of course not! We turn to those people who have experience! They've seen God's faithfulness in the storm. They've made it through to the other side.

Perseverance produces character, and character produces hope.

A Confident Hope

Hope, the Bible says, is "an anchor of the soul" (Heb. 6:19). It is the confident expectation of coming goodness. Without God, without faith in Jesus, we can't have hope. There is no expectation of coming goodness. Suffering is a part of life. There is no hope apart from Christ. He paved the way for us to enter God's inner sanctuary, to experience life more abundantly. A life filled with hope and joy. Hope is the confident expectation He is working all things together for our good and that he has gone before us to prepare a place for us to be with Him in eternity. He is with us, comforting us during our trials, and fighting our battles. We have hope because of what He has done for us. "He who did not spare His own Son, but delivered Him up for us all, how shall He not with Him also freely give us all things?" (Rom. 8:32)

"Now hope does not disappoint, because the love of God has been poured out in our hearts by the Holy Spirit who was given to us" (Rom. 5:5). *Hope will not lead to disappointment.* Of all the different emotions we experience during hard times, disappointment is the one that shows up the most during trials, isn't it? Disappointment in our spouse, disappointment in God, disappointment in ourselves, disappointment in our leaders, disappointment in our church. It seems like everyone has failed and we are left disappointed. But not God. He will never fail you.

Now you may be thinking, *You don't know what I've done. I've failed Him! I don't deserve anything!* or, *You don't know what I've been through! God has disappointed me!* Friend, I have felt the same. But the truth is, you didn't do anything to deserve God's goodness in the first place. The Bible says He died for you while you were still a sinner. "For when we were still without strength, in due time Christ died for the ungodly" (Rom. 5:6). There's nothing you can do to earn His continued goodness towards you. That's grace—God's unmerited favor. There's nothing you've done that deserves God's blessing, in fact, quite the opposite. That's mercy—not getting what you deserve. This is a promise I hold tightly to, "If we are faithless, He remains faithful; He cannot deny Himself" (2 Tim. 2:13).

Hope will not lead to disappointment.

Much like the marred clay in the Potter's hand, God promises He will complete the good work He has begun within you. The Potter is not going to leave you unfinished on the wheel. He promises to continue molding and shaping your life into the beautiful vessel He preplanned before the foundations of the earth. Writing to the Philippian church, Paul wrote, "being confident of this very thing, that He who has begun a good work in you will complete it until the day of Jesus Christ" (Phil. 1:6).

Vessels of Honor

Years ago, I had the privilege of watching the olive press working while visiting Israel. Following the crushing in the olive press, the olive paste is placed in baskets and pressed again, releasing its oil along with the most incredible aromas. This is what tribulations do in your life—they press and crush, until you exude the aroma of Christ Jesus. Friend, we can rejoice in our trials and suffering because our tribulations are working for us. As the Potter presses, shapes, and molds us, as He takes our marred clay and begins to reshape it again, and again, we will begin to let off the fragrance of the pressed life—the aroma of Christ.

The beauty of the olive press and the Potter's wheel is the finished product. The olive oil of highest quality, the finished vessel. The crushing and the shaping is not fun, nor easy. But it is necessary. The press is necessary to create the oil, and the pressing of the Potter's hands is necessary to shape the vessel. God's desire is to bring you to a place of spiritual maturity. The finished product is your life— even in times of hardship—exuding the aroma of Christ. Your life bringing the comfort of the Holy Spirit to people who don't know Him. That only happens if you go through the pressing. It's a choice to respond to loving hands of the Potter. Paul wrote, "But indeed, O man, who are you to reply against God? Will the thing formed say to him who formed it, 'Why have you made me like this?'" (Rom. 9:20)

We can rejoice because we know our current sufferings aren't worthy to be compared to the glory that is coming. We can rejoice because our trials are developing good things in our life. We can rejoice because we are safe in the Potter's hands. We can rejoice because He is working all things together for our good and His glory.

Yes, even this.

"But we have this treasure in earthen vessels, that the excellence of the power may be of God and not of us." (2 Cor. 4:7)

CHAPTER 7

SOMETIMES JESUS SENDS US INTO THE STORM

There are times when our trials are one test right after the other. The storms keep rolling in. While we recover from the exhaustion and depletion of yesterday—tomorrow, with all its troubles has already arrived. Life doesn't promise downtime or an option to pause between hardships. It can feel unfair, and hurtful. *God, why would You allow this to happen? You know I barely survived the last storm!* We know God is with us, working all these things together for our good and His glory, but some days, it's hard to believe it. Some spiritual realities are hard to accept. We know them to be true, but we don't understand.

Sometimes, Jesus leads us into the storm.

Following what was, up to that point, one of the greatest tests of their faith—the disciples found themselves in such a storm. Jesus had just fed a crowd of five-thousand men with a small boy's lunch—five loaves of bread and two fish. Some estimate with women and children, the number was closer to fifteen or twenty-thousand people. According to Philip, even if there was a local place where they could have purchased that much food, it would have cost well over two months wages to feed them all. It was impossible. It was incredible. And it was exhausting. While the fish and loaves were miraculously multiplying, the disciples were busy distributing the food to the huge crowd that had gathered. It was such an incredible miracle, when the crowd realized what had happened, they exclaimed, "This is truly the Prophet who is to come into the world" (John 6:14). They were ready to take Him by force and make Him their king.

The people of Israel desperately wanted to be rescued from the oppression of the Roman government. When they saw Jesus they thought, *Surely, He will be the one to deliver us from our bondage! He will deliver Israel and overthrow the Roman government!* Imagine if Jesus showed up in the middle of our broken, politically-torn, and hurting world today, preaching a gospel of peace and performing miracles that really helped people. Wouldn't we try to force Him into the presidency or some other form of leadership? The people of Israel knew the promise of a coming Savior, but they only saw Jesus for what He could do for them in the moment. They wanted political freedom. They misunderstood why they needed a Messiah. Jesus didn't come to overthrow the Roman government but to overthrow the power of sin in an unforgiven life.

Jesus came for a much greater reason than an oppressive government. He came to save our souls.

Into the Storm

"Now when evening came, His disciples went down to the sea, got into the boat, and went over the sea toward Capernaum. And it was already dark, and Jesus had not come to them. Then the sea arose because a great wind was blowing" (John 6:16-18). Matthew gives us a few more details about how it was that they found themselves on the lake encompassed by a great storm. Immediately after the miraculous feeding of the crowd, "Jesus made His disciples get into the boat and go before Him to the other side, while He sent the multitudes away. And when He had sent the multitudes away, He went up on the mountain by Himself to pray. Now when evening came, He was alone there" (Matt. 14:22-23).

The disciples were emotionally and spiritually exhausted from feeding twenty-thousand people. They heard the plans, the rumors—*Let's make Jesus our king!* Maybe they were overwhelmed by what they had just seen and heard. Perhaps they were frightened. Jesus *made them* get into the boat. He *made them* go without Him to the other side. Into the storm. The Sea of Galilee is actually a lake. It's about thirteen miles by eight miles, and nearly seven-hundred feet below sea level. It's surrounded by mountains, more like hills, from which you can observe the entire Sea of Galilee. While the disciples were out on the Sea of Galilee, Jesus retreated to one of the hilltops to pray.

Why would Jesus send His disciples—tired and worn out from the testing of their faith—directly into another test? Why would Jesus retreat to a hilltop to pray, knowing His disciples were heading toward a storm? We know God uses trials and tribulations to mold us. We know He is working all things together for our good and His glory. And sometimes, God sends us into a storm. A storm sovereignly designed for our good and His glory. This seems counterintuitive, doesn't it? We want to avoid storms, suffering, and hardship at all costs. But God's ways are not our ways. God says, "For as the heavens are higher than the earth, so are My ways higher than your ways, and My thoughts than your thoughts" (Isa. 55:9). So we need to ask ourselves a few questions. Did Jesus know there was going to be a storm on the Sea of Galilee? Did Jesus know there would be a mighty storm?

Yes, He did.

God knew there was a storm coming. God, in His sovereignty, sent them into the storm. God also knew there were lions in the den when Daniel was thrown in for remaining faithful in prayer to God. God knew there was a fiery furnace being prepared for those who refused to bow down to Nebuchadnezzar. He knew

Shadrach, Meshach, and Abednego would remain faithful to God and refuse to bow down. He knew they'd be thrown in. Why would God knowingly allow His children to walk into storms? The answer, my friends, is, for our good and His glory.

The Gospel of John tells the story of man who was born blind. At the time, it was commonly believed that a physical ailment such as this was an indication of sin. And so they asked Jesus why the man had been born blind. Was it because of his sins or the sins of his parents? "Jesus answered, 'Neither this man nor his parents sinned, but that the works of God should be revealed in him.'" (John 9:3)

Yes, God knew there was a storm coming. And yes, God sent the disciples into the storm. It's so easy for us to forget when we're in storm survival mode—*God also knew Jesus would show up to rescue them.* He knew He would shut the mouths of the lions for Daniel. He knew Jesus would show up in the fiery furnace with Shadrach, Meshach, and Abednego. He knew Jesus would heal the man born blind and God's power would be revealed in him. It's all for our good and His glory. I imagine Jesus sitting up on the hillside praying, with one eye open watching the disciples the entire time. He knew He would come and rescue them. He knew how it was going to end.

God hasn't forgotten about you, friend. He knows how it's going to end.

Correcting, Perfecting, and Protecting Storms

In the Scriptures, we see believers go through all different types of storms. You may recall the story of Jonah and the great fish, found in the book of Jonah. God called Jonah to go to Nineveh and tell of God's coming judgement for their sins. He was supposed to preach the gospel to them. Instead, he bought a ticket on a boat going in the opposite direction. He ran away, or boated away, as far as he could in disobedience to God. If you're familiar with the story, you know what happens next.

"But the Lord sent out a great wind on the sea, and there was a mighty tempest on the sea, so that the ship was about to be broken up. Then the mariners were afraid; and every man cried out to his god, and threw the cargo that was in the ship into the sea, to lighten the load. But Jonah had gone down into the lowest parts of the ship, had lain down, and was fast asleep." (Jon. 1:4-5)

Even the experienced mariners were desperate and afraid for their lives? That's quite a storm! This storm was sovereignly designed by God to get Jonah back on the right track for his life. The storm we find Jonah in is for his good and God's glory. I call this a *correcting storm*. We don't criticize a father for discipling his children. He does it because he loves them. He does it to protect them from future harm. God the Father loves you more.

Correcting storms are designed by God to get you back where you need to be. These types of storms are typically a direct result of sin on your part. Maybe you've found yourself in a complete mess by your own design. A correcting storm may look like the natural consequences we face as a result of our sin. They aren't punishment, they are corrections. Remember, God loves you. He is working all things together for your good and His glory. When you step outside of God's will for your life, you place yourself outside of the promises and protection of God.

As the sailors panicked, Jonah confessed the storm was a result of his own disobedience. He instructed them to throw him overboard to save themselves. The sailors were wary to do so, but in the end, they did. The first chapter of Jonah ends with this shocking statement: "Now the Lord had prepared a great fish to swallow Jonah. And Jonah was in the belly of the fish three days and three nights." (Jon. 1:17)

God's grace is the storm that comes as a result of your own sinful mistakes. God's mercy is the fish that swallows you when you're in the midst that storm. God not only prepared a fish to swallow Jonah, He also caused the fish to be sick—literally, to vomit Jonah up on the shores of Nineveh. He is always working for your good and His glory.

Perfecting storms are the storms God allows in our lives to teach us a lesson. Joseph's story is a great example of this. Joseph was the kind of young man all parents want to raise. In the totality of Joseph's life, the Bible doesn't mention anything about ungodliness or sinfulness. And yet, Joseph experienced great difficulty during his life. He had family difficulty. He had personal difficulty. He was falsely accused of great and horrendous sins. He was forgotten and abandoned. The storms God allowed in Joseph's life were perfecting him. They were molding and shaping Joseph into the kind of man who would lead the nation of Egypt and save the nation of Israel during a worldwide famine.

Perfecting storms are challenging to navigate because like Joseph, we don't know what God's end goal is. We don't understand why we have to go through the storm. We question God's faithfulness and wonder when it will be over. Imagine what Joseph must have thought over the years as he was sold into slavery, falsely accused of attempted rape, and thrown into prison as an innocent man. That's why hope is so important in the life of a believer. Hope is what keeps our soul anchored to the truths of heaven when suffering is weighing us down: God does love us. He is working all things together for our good and His glory. He has not forgotten us. None of us are so far gone He can't save us. He has a plan and it is good.

The third type of storm is what I personally believe the disciples were experiencing—*protecting storms*. The crowd gathered around Jesus was ready to make Him their king right then and there. There is no doubt the disciples themselves had wondered at the kingdom

Jesus was bringing. Would it be earthly as well as heavenly? James and John would later argue over who would sit next to Jesus in His kingdom. In the garden of Gethsemane, Peter pulled out his sword as if to protect Jesus and His kingdom by force.

Jesus removed the disciples from the frenzy of the crowd and placed them in a storm for their own protection. Who knows what would have happened if the disciples had remained with the crowd? Protecting storms are designed, as you would guess, for our protection. Perhaps, like the disciples, we've just experienced an incredible miracle. Rather than leave us where we might be tempted to take credit or to get caught up in the frenzy, God removes and protects us with a storm. Protecting storms build and refine our faith.

Trouble on the Sea

"But the boat was now in the middle of the sea, tossed by the waves, for the wind was contrary. Now in the fourth watch of the night Jesus went to them, walking on the sea. And when the disciples saw Him walking on the sea, they were troubled, saying, 'It is a ghost!' And they cried out for fear." (Matt. 14:24-26)

The disciples were in trouble. John fills us in on a few more details. The winds were so strong, that in all this time—the time since Jesus had sent the disciples into the boat and slipped away to pray until three o'clock in the morning—they had only rowed three or four miles (John 6:15-21). These were experienced fishermen. Some of them had grown up fishing the Sea of Galilee. They could handle a storm. But at three o'clock in the morning, while Jesus was praying, they were in trouble.

Some storms seem to go on forever. Like the disciples, we've been rowing and rowing and have only gone a few miles. Our strength is gone and we are in trouble. That's where the disciples were when Jesus came walking on the water. They were so immersed in the elements, the storm, and their own fear—*they didn't even recognize Him*. They thought He was a ghost. As strange as that sounds, I can identify with the disciples. I have experienced storms so severe that my vision—my recognition even of the things of God—was clouded. *Is that you, Lord? I can't tell.* "But immediately Jesus spoke to them, saying, 'Be of good cheer! It is I; do not be afraid.' And Peter answered Him and said, 'Lord, if it is You, command me to come to You on the water'" (Matt. 14:27-28).

Sometimes God waits until, like Peter, we are so desperate we cry out to Him.

For those of you going through the storm, wondering where Jesus is, wondering if He's coming, or if He knows how much trouble you're in—He is, and He does. Quite often, God is waiting for us to invite Him into the boat. He's praying for you with one eye open watching you. He's waiting for you to be desperate enough to cry out to Him for help. God will not force Himself upon you. He will not force Himself into your life. If you aren't asking for His help, if you don't want His help—He's not going to force it on you. His help is available to you the moment you ask, but He will not force you to take it. God is waiting for you to invite Him into your life, your challenges, and the storm you've found yourself in.

Peter cried out to Jesus in the middle of the storm and Jesus answered, "'Come'" (Matt. 14:29).

> "And when Peter had come down out of the boat, he walked on the water to go to Jesus. But when he saw that the wind was boisterous, he was afraid; and beginning to sink he cried out, saying, 'Lord, save me!' And immediately Jesus stretched out His hand and caught him, and said to him, 'O you of little faith, why did you doubt?' And when they got into the boat, the wind ceased. Then those who were in the boat came and worshiped Him, saying, 'Truly You are the Son of God.'" (Matt. 14:29-33)

Yes, God knew there was a storm coming. And yes, He knew He would rescue them.

Come

After the death and resurrection of Jesus, two of His followers walked along the road heading toward the town of Emmaus. They had heard of Jesus' death but did not yet know of His resurrection. Peter and John had discovered the empty tomb earlier that day, but did not understand what it meant. The two disciples on the road to Emmaus were deeply sad and talking of recent events as they walked. All of their hopes had just died on a cross.

As they talked, Jesus appeared and walked with them, but God kept them from recognizing Him. Jesus asked, "'What kind of conversation is this that you have with one another as you walk and are sad?'" (Luke 24:17). They couldn't believe this man had not yet heard the news about Jesus. They told Him the whole story of what Jesus had done, who they thought He had been, and of His death.

Jesus then explained to them from the scriptures how the Messiah would suffer before He entered into glory. About this time, they were nearly at their destination of Emmaus. Jesus acted as though He was going further on the road, but the two disciples begged him to stay with them. And so He did. "Now it came to pass, as He sat at the table with them, that He took bread, blessed and broke it, and gave it to them. Then their eyes were opened and they knew Him; and He vanished from their sight." (Luke 24:30-31)

Jesus waited until the two followers invited Him into their story, into their lives. Jesus waited until the disciples cried out to Him for help. And Jesus will wait for you too, to call out to Him, "Lord, come."

I often wonder what Peter was thinking when he called out to Jesus to invite him onto the water. He didn't say, "Lord, if it's really You, get in this boat right now!" He said, "Lord, if it is You, command me to come to You on the water" (Matt. 14:28). I wonder if this was Peter's way of saying, "Lord, if it's really You, You could make this storm into something good. You could call me out onto the waves—to rise above the storm and walk on the water."

I believe God would extend that same invitation to each of us today. To you who are tired of rowing, afraid of the storm, anxious about what will happen next, soaked and chilled from the waves, wondering if God will give you the strength to walk on the water . . . when you call out to Jesus, He says, "Come."

"But those who wait on the Lord shall renew their strength; they shall mount up with wings like eagles, they shall run and not be weary, they shall walk and not faint." (Isa. 40:31)

CHAPTER 8

FROM BITTERNESS TO BETTERNESS

There are some trials so great we describe the rest of our lives by what happened before . . . and after. The tragedy that altered everything. The crisis that left you reeling. The incident you wished had never happened. These moments always bring us to a crossroad—a place of decision. We cannot go back to the way things were. We cannot gain back what we've lost. We cannot remain where we are, but moving forward feels impossible. We've had the wind knocked out of us and we aren't able to make sense of it all, much less get up and move on. The Proverbs say, "A man's steps are of the LORD; How then can a man understand his own way?" (Prov. 20:24)

The book of Ruth is a story of God's providence, God's protection, and promises. It's a story of how God sovereignly takes the events of our lives and weaves them together for His will. Where we live, who we marry, where we travel. He takes the tragedies and the successes. He takes the hopelessness and infuses hope.

The book of Ruth begins with a man named Elimelech, and his wife Naomi. In this story, the names of the people and places are important. *Elimelech's* name means "my God is king."[10] *Naomi* means "pleasant or my delight."[11] Elimelech, along with Naomi and their two sons lived in *Bethlehem*, or "House of Bread," in the region of Judah, Israel.[12]

Although Elimelech's king was God, and although he lived in the House of Bread, when a severe famine fell upon the land, he moved his family to the country of Moab, a place that hated God. While in Moab, Elimelech died. Their sons both married Moabite women, *Orpah*—"Gazelle,"[13] and *Ruth*—"Friendship."[14] But nearly ten years later, both of Naomi's sons died as well. Summing up the most devastating ten years of her life, the Bible says, "so the woman survived her two sons and her husband" (Ruth 1:5).

What was intended to save their family—a move to escape the famine and find food—became tragedy after tragedy, dramatically changing Naomi's entire future. She was a widow. A mother without her children. A foreigner. A woman with no protection, provision, or prospects. She had no family left except the two women her sons had married. It was a tragedy of epic proportions. She had lost everything.

Her life would never be the same.

No doubt, Naomi felt angry, hurt, and forgotten by God. Warren Wiersbe wrote, "Because God gave us freedom of choice, we can ignore the will of God, argue with it, disobey it, even fight against it. But in the end, the will of God shall prevail."[15] I'm sure Naomi did argue with the will of God, or at least wondered if they shouldn't have come to Moab in the first place. *What if Elimelech hadn't decided to run away from our problems to this God-hating country of Moab? What if we would have stayed in Bethlehem and waited out the famine? Would I still have lost everything?* I've wondered at the will of God myself, as I'm sure you have too.

Trials and difficulties, troubles and hardships, always leave us a choice to make. And sometimes, more than one. We can take matters into our own hands and try to solve it ourselves; we can run away from or avoid our problems like Elimelech; or we can embrace the trials of life and trust Jesus through them, allowing Him to be our strength and our wisdom. It's a choice to believe God still has a future hope for you in spite of loss. This is where we find Naomi in the first chapter of Ruth. After hearing the famine in Bethlehem had ended and the Lord had blessed His people with food, she must decide how to move forward.

Naomi is a great example of how many of us feel. She decides to head back to Bethlehem. She's going to push on, but she isn't ready to embrace her life just yet. She's still hurting, still grieving. That's where many of us find ourselves today. We've survived the tragedy, but we aren't thriving yet. We have turned back toward the House of Bread, but our heart isn't there yet. Let me offer you this encouragement today—we don't need to be completely healed to get back up and keep going. We don't need to have all the details worked out in order to start heading to the House of Bread, to the place where God is King. Grief is a process, just like healing is a process. It takes time, and usually happens when we aren't looking.

The Trouble with Bitterness

Naomi begins the journey back to Judah, along with her two daughters-in-law, Ruth and Orpah. But along the way, she changes her mind and tries to send them back home to their families in Moab. "'Go, return each to her mother's house. The Lord deal kindly with you, as you have dealt with the dead and with me. The Lord grant that you may find rest, each in the house of her husband'" (Ruth 1:8-9).

But Ruth and Orpah would not leave Naomi. They cried and begged Naomi to take them with her. Naomi wouldn't hear of it. "Look, don't come with me, I don't plan on getting married again; I don't plan on having children again, and even if I had children, would you wait for them all these years so that you could marry them and have a life? Just go! I cannot do anything for you anymore!" (Ruth 1:10-13, author's paraphrase)

Like so many of us do when we're hurting, Naomi limited herself to her own abilities. She describes a future based within the realm of what she believes is humanly possible. She's forgotten God her King is limitless. She's so stuck in her grief, she even believes God is against her. "'No, my daughters; for it grieves me very much for your sakes that the hand of the Lord has gone out against me!'" (Ruth 1:13) Naomi isn't speaking or thinking like a spiritual woman. When we don't go to God with our grief and suffering—we begin to sound like people who don't believe in God.

Little did Naomi know, God had a plan to use one of these daughters-in-law to show His faithfulness to her. Ruth, the one she tried to leave behind, was actually God's plan to bless Naomi. God was already preparing a place of great blessing for her. "But as it is written: 'Eye has not seen, nor ear heard, nor have entered into the heart of man the things which God has prepared for those who love Him'" (1 Cor. 2:9). This promise is true for all of us who love God.

If you are in a place of grief, or still struggling to get up from your latest tragedy, be encouraged. God is sovereignly weaving together all of the details of your life for your good and His glory. Even the ill-advised trip to the place outside of God's blessings. Even the things you said in grief, the people in your life you tried to cancel out. God is using all of it for your good and His glory. The place of blessing He is preparing for you is beyond what you could possibly imagine.

But we must choose to believe it's true.

The trouble with bitterness is it robs us of our hope. What starts out as a small offense—whether with God like Naomi, or with someone else—takes root in our hearts and begins to inform our decisions and our attitudes. Eventually, it robs us of our hope and joy. That unforgiveness leads to resentment, and resentment grows and becomes bitterness. Bitterness takes root when we stew on the offense. When we refuse to run to God with our hurts—even when we believe He is the one who has hurt us. One of the hardest things to do when someone is grieving, or when we ourselves are grieving, is to acknowledge sin. We offer compassion and understanding, as we should! But we must remember those feelings of hurt and betrayal, if not brought before the Lord can turn into unforgiveness, resentment, and bitterness. It will lead us to make decisions, like Naomi, outside the will of God—without prayer, without biblical counsel.

The Proverbs say, "He who covers his sins will not prosper, but whoever confesses and forsakes them will have mercy" (Prov. 28:13). It's never a good idea for us to cover our sin with excuses on why we can't or won't do something. In Naomi's case, it would have been better for her to repent and humble herself before the mighty hand of God. To cry out to God. Why, God? *Why have You taken my husband and my children from me? Why have You left me alone? Do You not care about me? Are You against me?* Consider, even in asking these hard questions of God, it would open the door for a conversation. Instead, she simply states God is against her.

God wants to restore the joy that bitterness has stolen from you. He wants to restore the hope in the future of blessings He has planned for you. Suffering and difficulties steal those things as they are a result of sin in this fallen world. But God's heart is to restore and renew. To fill you with hope, joy, and peace once again. "This hope we have as an anchor of the soul, both sure and steadfast, and which enters the Presence behind the veil, where the forerunner has entered for us, even Jesus" (Heb. 6:19).

As we'll see with Naomi, although she's still bitter, God is already moving her in the direction of the place where He will bless her with hope and joy beyond her wildest dreams. What she never thought possible—the things she said would never happen—are going to happen. Jesus said, "With men it is impossible, but not with God; for with God all things are possible" (Mark 10:27).

Don't Call Me Pleasant

In spite of Naomi's repeated discouragement, Ruth refused to leave her. Orpah kissed Naomi and returned to her family in Moab. But the Bible says Ruth clung to Naomi, saying:

> "Entreat me not to leave you, or to turn back from following after you; for wherever you go, I will go; and wherever you lodge, I will lodge; your people shall be my people, and your God, my God. Where you die, I will die, and there will I be buried. The Lord do so to me, and more also, if anything but death parts you and me." (Ruth 1:16-17)

As a pastor, I am often asked to read these verses when performing a wedding ceremony. They are beautiful words of commitment between two people who love each other. But this covenant here in its original context, is really a promise between two widows to become one family. This is a wonderful example of the type of covenant that God intends for His family, for the church, the body of Christ. This is the type of commitment we are to have towards one another as fellow believers, as family in Christ—to support and stand by one another through good times and bad times.

God blessed Naomi in spite of herself and in spite of her bitterness.

Ruth and Naomi continued together on their journey together to Bethlehem. When they arrived, the women of Bethlehem were excited and surprised to see Naomi. They asked each other, "'Is this Naomi?'" (Ruth1:19). *Is it really Naomi? Is this Pleasant? Has Pleasant finally returned home?!*

> "But she said to them, 'Do not call me Naomi; call me Mara, for the Almighty has dealt very bitterly with me. I went out full, and the Lord has brought me home again empty. Why do you call me Naomi, since the Lord has testified against me, and the Almighty has afflicted me?'" (Ruth 1:20-21)

The name *Mara*, in Hebrew, means "bitterness."[16] She's saying, *Don't call me Pleasant, call me Bitterness.* In my many years of ministering to people who are grieving and hurting, I have yet to run into someone so bold they would say, "Just call me bitterness." Usually they try to hide it, or put a good face on it. They call it sarcasm or cynicism. But it's neither of those things. It's an offense or a hurt that has rooted itself so deeply within their heart it's grown into resentment and bitterness. So often in times of death, we blame God—especially for those deaths we believe to be untimely. Let me just say this— death always feels untimely. Age doesn't matter. Contribution to society don't matter. It always feels out of place. The Bible declares death is an enemy that Christ defeated through the cross and His resurrection.

Death always feels wrong because God did not create us for death. He created us for eternal life in His Son, Jesus Christ. We must remember—before sin entered the world, there was no death. Death is a result of sin, the root of all suffering is sin, and yet God's will—in spite of sin, death, and destruction—always prevails. And God's will for you is good. His plans for you are good. He is able to use even the horrible, tragic things that have happened in your life to accomplish His will.

Naomi wasn't the only person in the Bible who blamed God for the death of a loved one. In the book of John, we learn of a family, siblings—Mary, Martha and Lazarus—all of whom knew Jesus and all of whom Jesus loved. When Lazarus became sick, they called for Jesus to come hopeful that He would heal their brother. But Jesus delayed, and Lazarus died. When Jesus finally arrived in Bethany, Martha ran out to Him, crying out, "Lord, if You had been here, my brother would not have died" (John 11:21). Martha blamed Jesus for the death of her brother. Naomi wasn't the first, nor will she be the last person to blame God. Blame is a normal response to grief.

The book of Hebrews exhorts us, to look "carefully lest anyone fall short of the grace of God; lest any root of bitterness springing up cause trouble, and by this many become defiled" (Heb. 12:15). The temptation when we're hurting, or grieving is to blame God because our circumstances have changed. It's so easy for us when things don't go our way, or when things are bad, to think God is mean, He's forgotten us, He's vindictive, or He doesn't love us. But it's not true. God's love for you hasn't changed. God's plan for you hasn't changed. Only your circumstances have changed.

Bitterness will keep you from experiencing the grace and comfort of God within your suffering, the moment when you need it the most.

When we grieve and sorrow over death, we are really grieving our loss. Our loved ones who knew God are in a better place. They are where we all desire to be—a place with no more sorrow, and no more tears. Looking into the face of Jesus. Known completely as they are. No longer misunderstood, broken, or in pain. Their last breath on earth led to their first breath in the presence of God. They just arrived at their final destination a little earlier than us, and so, we are the ones who sorrow. But not without hope.

"But I do not want you to be ignorant, brethren, concerning those who have fallen asleep, lest you sorrow as others who have no hope. Then we who are alive and remain shall be caught up together with them in the clouds to meet the Lord in the air. And thus we shall always be with the Lord." (1 Thess. 4:13, 17)

The Cure for Mara

When Naomi and Ruth arrived in Bethlehem, it was the time of harvest. Ruth went into the fields to find grain left behind by the harvesters for she and Naomi. "And she happened to come to the part of the field belonging to Boaz, who was of the family of Elimelech" (Ruth 2:3b). Boaz was the kinsman redeemer of Naomi's

76

family—a male relative whose duty it was to redeem the property of those too poor to claim it; to redeem one who had sold themselves into slavery; or to redeem a family by marrying a widow and raising a son in the name of her dead husband.

Boaz fell in love with and married Ruth, a foreigner and a widow, redeeming all of Elimelech's property and raising up another son for Naomi. Naomi went away full, and returned home empty, but God already had a plan to redeem her losses and restore her future.

King David wrote in the Psalms:

> "Bless the LORD, O my soul; and all that is within me, bless His holy name! Bless the LORD, O my soul, and forget not all His benefits: Who forgives all your iniquities, who heals all your diseases, who redeems your life from destruction, who crowns you with lovingkindness and tender mercies, who satisfies your mouth with good things, so that your youth is renewed like the eagle's." (Ps. 103:1-5)

In Exodus, God said, "I am the Lord; I will bring you out from under the burdens of the Egyptians, I will rescue you from their bondage, and I will redeem you with an outstretched arm and with great judgments" (Exod. 6:6). Jesus is our Kinsman Redeemer. He has redeemed us from the curse of death and slavery to sin. He heals all of the curses and suffering sin has brought into our lives.

In the book of Exodus, Moses writes of the journey the children of Israel took following their escape from years of slavery in the land of Egypt. The children of Israel passed through the Red Sea and worshipped God for faithfully delivering them from their enemies. Then they continued on their journey. "Now when they came to Marah, they could not drink the waters of Marah, for they were bitter. Therefore the name of it was called Marah. And the people complained against Moses, saying, 'What shall we drink?'" (Exod. 15:23-24)

Marah. It's the same Hebrew word Naomi used to describe herself.

"So he cried out to the Lord, and the Lord showed him a tree. When he cast it into the waters, the waters were made sweet" (Ex. 15:25).

God's solution to the bitter water, His solution for our complaining, hurting hearts, is a tree. God has provided a tree for you and me, too. It's a piece of wood in the shape of a cross—the cross of Jesus Christ. God's cure for bitterness is forgiveness. It's the forgiveness we receive from God through the sacrifice of Jesus on the cross for us. It's the forgiveness we extend to each other—whether or not its deserved—that brings healing to our bitter and hurting hearts. It was there at the bitter water that God declared, "I am the Lord who heals you" (Ex. 15:26), because it wasn't just the bitter water that needed healing that day—it was all of us too.

> "Then the women said to Naomi, 'Blessed be the Lord, who has not left you this day without a close relative; and may his name be famous in Israel! And may he be to you a restorer of life and a nourisher of your old age; for your daughter-in-law, who loves you, who is better to you than seven sons, has borne him.' Then Naomi took the child and laid him on her bosom, and became a nurse to him. Also the neighbor women gave him a name, saying, 'There is a son born to Naomi.' And they called his name Obed. He is the father of Jesse, the father of David." (Ruth 4:14-17)

Obed became the father of Jesse, who became the father of King David. King David became the many times great-grandfather of the King of all kings, Jesus Christ. When you and I choose to walk in the forgiveness of God, even our most bitter waters are made sweet by the redemptive cross of Jesus.

> *"Then Jesus said to His disciples, 'If anyone desires to come after Me, let him deny himself, and take up his cross, and follow Me.'"*
> (Matt. 16:24)

CHAPTER 9

YES, EVEN IN THAT

Jacob, who was later renamed Israel, learned things the hard way. Jacob's name means "heel catcher" or "supplanter," because while he was still in the womb, he struggled with his twin brother and during delivery reached out and grabbed his brother's heel.[17] The word supplanter is not one we hear every day. It means "to supersede (another) especially by force or treachery."[18] Jacob was always trying to get ahead, and often at the expense of those around him. He was a manipulator most of his life.

In his younger years, Jacob convinced his twin brother Esau to trade his birthright for a bowl of soup, and later tricked his father Isaac into giving him the blessing reserved for Esau. When Esau discovered what Jacob had done, he threatened to kill him. And so, encouraged by his mother, Jacob fled to Paddan-aram to escape his brother's wrath and to find a wife amongst his mother's family. Jacob was always wrestling with God and manipulating to get ahead, because *he didn't really believe that God was for him.* He learned to trust God the hard way.

But God met Jacob while he was running away, and God met Jacob again years later on his way back home.

In Genesis 42, we find an older Jacob, reaping the harvest of the sinful mistakes of his youth—all those years of putting himself first and not trusting God. His favorite son Joseph is gone. We know he's been sold into slavery by his brothers, but Jacob doesn't know that. He believes Joseph is dead. His oldest son Ruben has disgraced him. His son Judah has been dishonored, and his daughter Dinah defiled. His son Simeon is in prison. And his beloved wife Rachel, has died. On top of all this, there's a famine in the land. He's facing the reality of starvation, not only for himself, but for his entire family.

And it gets worse.

The Egyptian Pharaoh's second-in-command—the same one who imprisoned Simeon—is now demanding Jacob send his youngest son, Benjamin, to Egypt in exchange for Simeon's freedom. Jacob is undone. He's overwhelmed. Life has punched him in the gut one too many times and now they want his baby, Benjamin. Not only was Benjamin the last son from his wife Rachel, but when Joseph disappeared, Benjamin took over as Jacob's favorite. He couldn't bear to part with Benjamin. Jacob exclaimed to his sons, "You have bereaved me: Joseph is no more, Simeon is no more, and you want to take Benjamin. All these things are against me"(Gen. 42:36). Jacob couldn't see a positive resolution for all of his suffering. No silver lining. No possible happy ending.

Jacob believed everything was against him—including God.

Jacob's sons would later become the patriarchs of Israel, a nation set apart for God. But they too, would learn things the hard way. In Jeremiah 29, the nation of Israel was under the captive rule of Babylon. They had chosen idolatry over worshipping the true God, and personal gain over taking care of the land God had given them. Although God had warned Israel to turn back to Him, they did not listen.

As a result of the Babylonian captivity, families were torn apart, people were carted away to foreign lands, and many were left behind starving. It was such a deep time of suffering, they began to believe God must be against them. They couldn't see anything good in their situation. They didn't think they would ever see God's blessings again. But during this terrible time, God spoke to them.

"For I know the thoughts that I think toward you, says the Lord, thoughts of peace and not of evil, to give you a future and a hope. Then you will call upon Me and go and pray to Me, and I will listen to you. And you will seek Me and find Me, when you search for Me with all your heart." (Jer. 29:11-13)

Grace in the Wilderness

Feelings can easily deceive us, can't they? Jacob's feelings were real, but he was wrong. God was not against him. His circumstances were not designed to harm him, as much as they hurt him. The Bible says, "The heart is deceitful above all things, and desperately wicked; who can know it?" (Jer. 17:9) Our heart, our feelings—especially when we are suffering—can deceive us. Our feelings, just like Jacob's, are real. But the conclusions they bring us to are often wrong.

It isn't good to make big decisions when you're in the midst of grief or suffering—your feelings will often lead you to make bad decisions or come to incorrect conclusions. Like Jacob and the nation of Israel, we mistakenly conclude God is against us. Many of us have lived our lives like Jacob and the nation of Israel. We have put ourselves first and forgotten God. We have believed everything is against us, that God is against us as we walked through times of suffering—and possibly the consequences of our own sinful choices. We have believed God has abandoned us.

Tough times can cause us to lose heart and lose sight of eternity. Intense trials and painful events cause us to lose sight of God and

His purposes for our lives. As Paul taught us earlier in the book of Romans, "For I consider that the sufferings of this present time are not worthy to be compared with the glory which shall be revealed in us" (Rom. 8:18). We must hold tightly to our heavenly perspective.

Paul reminds us in 2 Corinthians, "Therefore we do not lose heart. Even though our outward man is perishing, yet the inward man is being renewed day by day. For our light affliction, which is but for a moment, **is working for us** a far more exceeding and eternal weight of glory" (2 Cor. 4:16-17, emphasis added). Our afflictions are working *for us*, not against us. They are working for us a far more exceeding and eternal weight of glory. As we look at our trials through a biblical lens, by faith we see there is purpose in our pain. There is an end coming where we will understand how all the pieces come together.

God is for us—not against us.

There are so many things we have no control over in life; where we were born, to whom we were born, where we were educated, our economic status. These are things we can't choose for ourselves, and yet, God uses them. The choices of our parents (addiction, abuse, divorce), whether someone likes us or hates us, whether our family will help us or hurt us, whether our friends will be loyal or betray us, or if our spouse will stay with us. These things are outside of our control. But they aren't outside of God's control.

As a pastor, I've been asked many times, "Can you explain why this is happening to me? What good can God possibly work through this?" And the truth is, I don't know. But even if I could offer you some clarification, would it really satisfy you? Would a simple explanation alleviate you of all the pain and suffering you're experiencing? Would you agree to endure the pain if you knew exactly what God was doing? I would argue, no. No, you wouldn't. None of us want to suffer. What we're really looking for isn't an explanation, but something to relieve our pain. We are looking for comfort.

In Jeremiah 31, God spoke again to the children of Israel in exile, "'The people who survived the sword found grace in the wilderness—Israel, when I went to give him rest. The Lord has appeared of old to me, saying: 'Yes, I have loved you with an everlasting love; Therefore with lovingkindness I have drawn you'" (Jer. 31:2-3). God was telling the children of Israel, "I love you. Even in your time in Babylon. This is going to turn out for good, for your good. You're going to make it through. I'm going to use even this horrible time in your life for your good. You're going to be a better person because of it" (Jer. 31:2-3, my paraphrase). God is saying the same thing to you and me today. You're going to be better because of this trial in your life. And for others—you're already better because of that trial God allowed in your life. Those things you never would have chosen for yourself have become tools in the hand of a loving God, to give you a hope and a future.

Even if you're standing in the wilderness, you're going to find His grace.

And We Know

When we come to those things we don't understand, we need to fall back on the things we do understand. It's true, there are things we just don't know. We don't have all the answers, especially as they relate to our hurt and pain. But we must not give up the things we do know just for a few things we can't comprehend right now. One day we will understand. One day it will all be revealed and explained in the presence of the Lord. As Paul wrote to the Corinthians, "For now we see in a mirror, dimly, but then face to face. Now I know in part, but then I shall know just as I also am known." (1 Cor. 13:12)

"**And we know** that all things work together for good to those who love God, to those who are the called according to His purpose" (Rom. 8:28, emphasis added).

The phrase that Paul uses for *and we know,* in the original Greek language could also be translated, *and we know that we know that we know.* It's a statement of certainty, assurance, and confidence. There are some things in your life you know that you know that you know to be true. The sky is blue. The world is round. You love your kids. You know these things to be true. That's what Paul is saying here— and we know this to be true: God causes all things, everything, to work together for the good of those who love God. It's true for those of us who learn things the hard way. It's true for those of us who keep getting tripped up over the same sin. I don't always get it. I can't always see God's hand working behind the scenes. But I know that I know that I know it to be true: God is causing all of these things to work together for our good and His glory.

For some of us, we read Romans 8:28 and we think, *Really? All things?* Paul isn't saying that *all things are good.* They're not. He's saying that all things are *working together for our good and God's glory.* And there are some who don't really believe that. They can't fathom that God really is able to use even the horrific, tragic events they've experienced for their good and His glory. They read Romans 8:28 and think, *most things, or some things* work together for good, but certainly not *all things.* Like Jacob, they're making plans to take care of themselves. To work it out for their own good because it hurts too much to wait on the Lord, not knowing how it's going to end.

The psalmist said, "Wait on the Lord; be of good courage, and He shall strengthen your heart; wait, I say, on the Lord!" (Ps. 27:14) It takes courage to wait and trust God to work out even these painful moments in our lives for good. The Bible says we live by faith. "Now faith is the substance of things hoped for, the evidence of things not seen" (Heb. 11:1). When we use our spiritual eyes of faith, when we look at our situation from a spiritual perspective, we are able to trust God even in the darkness. Do you really think you could work out your situation for your good *and the good of every other believer involved who loves God?* Even with your best intentions, you can't possibly come up with a solution that's for the good of *all those who love God.* Only a sovereign God can do that. We need to trust He loves us and has good plans for us.

The world is filled with sorrows and difficulties. There are tragedies. Not everything goes our way or happens according to our plans. Our lives are filled with suffering and hardships. But we know this to be true: God is working all things together for our good and His glory. A believer who's been saved by the blood of Jesus Christ knows this. We may not always believe it. We may not always accept it. But we know it. God is causing all things to work together for your good and His glory. It was true for Jacob, it was true for the nation of Israel, and it's true for you, too. That person who is against you? God is going to work it out. That family you're not connected with? God is going to work it out. That hard situation you're facing at work? God is going to work it out for *your good.* He is working all of these things together for good and not for bad. God is not against you, and neither are the situations in your life, as heavy and hard as they are.

We aren't just victims of circumstance. Sin has negatively affected all of us—whether our own sins, the sins of others, or the result of living in a sinful, fallen world. But we are not victims. We are victors. We are conquerors.

"Yet in all these things we are more than conquerors through Him who loved us." (Rom. 8:37)

Yes, God is Working Even in That

Jacob believed everything was against him, even God. But he didn't know, he didn't understand—God was actually causing all of those things to work together for Jacob's good. The son Jacob thought was dead was alive! Joseph was alive! The second-in-command of Egypt holding Simeon in prison and demanding Benjamin come—*was Jacob's lost son, Joseph!* God already had a plan to save Jacob's family from the famine in the land! God wasn't trying to take Benjamin away from Jacob. God was drawing Jacob and Benjamin to Egypt to see the proof—He truly was working all things together for their good.

The children of Israel believed God was against them while they sat in Babylonian captivity for seventy years. The consequences for their sin felt too heavy to bear. They believed God had forsaken and forgotten them. They couldn't understand how God could work out even their forced captivity for their good and His glory. The promises from God during that time, the messages of hope from the prophet Jeremiah, probably sounded trite and even cliché. *Could God really work this together for our good? Nothing about this feels like God loves me. What future hope? We need help now!* They didn't see, they didn't understand, the future hope God was promising was so much bigger than just the restoration of their country.

James wrote, "Blessed is the man who endures temptation; for when he has been approved, he will receive the crown of life which the Lord has promised to those who love Him" (James 1:12). God was preparing Jacob, the children of Israel, and us—through testings and trials—for something better. They were longing for an earthly explanation, something to comfort them in their grief and loss. But God was working to not only prepare them for the miraculous return to their country on earth, but for a heavenly country. A family redeemed and restored by God's grace. A place for all those who love God. A place yet to come. Jacob did see the restoration of his family and the children of Israel did see the reunification of their country. And by faith, we will also see healing and restoration here on earth. But there is something coming that cannot be compared to any joy we may imagine in this world.

The Hall of Faith in the book of Hebrews gives Jacob special mention. Yes, Jacob—who spent his younger years wrestling with God and manipulating to get ahead. Yes, Jacob—who believed everything in his life, including God, was against him. Hebrews says, "By faith Jacob, when he was dying, blessed each of the sons of Joseph, and worshiped, leaning on the top of his staff" (Heb. 11:21). Jacob saw the proof of God's promises in Egypt when he met the son he thought was lost. When he met grandchildren he didn't know about and blessed them. Yes, even Jacob—who learned things the hard way—saw the hand of God working together all those things in his life for his good and God's glory.

And friend, it is by faith that you too can believe this promise: God is for you. He is causing all these things in your life—yes, even that—to work together for your good and His glory. You can trust Him.

"When the Lord brought back the captivity of Zion, we were like those who dream. Then our mouth was filled with laughter, and our tongue with singing. Then they said among the nations, 'The Lord has done great things for them.' The Lord has done great things for us, and we are glad. Bring back our captivity, O Lord, as the streams in the South. Those who sow in tears shall reap in joy. He who continually goes forth weeping, bearing seed for sowing, shall doubtless come again with rejoicing, bringing his sheaves with him." (Ps. 126:1-6)

CHAPTER 10

SOMETHING BETTER FOR US

It seems so strange that God would use suffering and pain—things no one wants to experience—as the vehicle for us to draw close to Him and one another. There is something in each of us that says, "I can do this on my own. I don't need anyone else." Or "This hurts too much. I want to be by myself." But we were not designed to live life alone. God created us for relationships, and most importantly, a relationship with Him.

When sin entered the world through the disobedience of Adam and Eve, suffering followed. Sin cut them off from intimacy with God. It ruined everything. Adam and Eve began hiding from God and from one another. With every subsequent generation, the brokenness continued. The burden of sin and suffering was too heavy for man to carry alone. And yet they continued to try to break free on their own. But it didn't work.

Even Moses, the man who brought the ten commandments down from Mount Sinai, experienced disappointment and loss. He sensed early on he was called by God to deliver the Children of Israel from Egypt. But he took matters into his own hands, killed a man, and spent forty years in the desert. In isolation. Alone. It was nothing like what he believed God had called him to do, or to be. And yet, God was at work during those years in the wilderness.

He was undoing everything Moses had learned about life in the previous forty years.

Moses did become a deliverer for the Children of Israel. After he led them out of Egypt, he spent another forty years back in the desert wilderness listening to them complain about how freedom wasn't what they thought it was going to be. I'm sure it didn't turn out the way Moses expected, either. The writer of Hebrews says this of Moses:

> "By faith Moses, when he became of age, refused to be called the son of Pharaoh's daughter, choosing rather to suffer affliction with the people of God than to enjoy the passing pleasures of sin, esteeming the reproach of Christ greater riches than the treasures in Egypt; for he looked to the reward." (Heb. 11:24-26)

Moses chose to share in the affliction of God's people *by faith*, because he believed there was something better for them—together.

Due to his own sin, Moses never entered the Promised Land. In fact, the book of Hebrews tells us many of the heroes of the faith did not receive all of God's promises here on earth. "And all these, having obtained a good testimony through faith, did not receive the promise, God having provided something better **for us**, that they should not be made perfect **apart from us**" (Heb. 11:39-40, emphasis added). Their life didn't turn out as they'd expected, or probably as they'd hoped. They pressed on anyway because they believed the glory to come would far outweigh any blessings they had here on earth. They reckoned there was something better ahead. They accepted by faith—God had something better in mind *for us*.

And they were right.

Better Together

The truth is, we need each other. We need the encouragement that comes from being together with other believers. The compassion we glean from seeing our Christian brothers and sisters walking through times of great difficulty. The reassurance to trust God that the journey is worth it; that He really is working these things together for good; that our pain means something; that our suffering has purpose.

We need to surround ourselves with other believers because we don't always see the bigger picture God is painting. We need to be encouraged to keep walking by faith when times are tough. It's not hard to worship God when there's money in the bank and everything is going your way, is it? We raise our hands and praise God because it feels good to be alive! But when we experience difficulties and tragedies, worship becomes an act of faith. We need others to help us lift our hands and voices as we proclaim in faith, we still believe in God's goodness. We still believe in God's ability to work all these things together for our good and His glory.

The book of Hebrews exhorts us,

> "And let us consider one another in order to stir up love and good works, not forsaking the assembling of ourselves together, as is the manner of some, but exhorting one another, and so much the more as you see the Day approaching." (Heb. 10:24-25)

Trials, difficulties, and pain tend to isolate us. We feel no one else understands, or we feel too vulnerable to be with others. But there is something about gathering together with other believers that builds us up. God has distributed unique spiritual gifts to each of us, activated specifically when we are in fellowship. Peter wrote, "As each one has received a gift, minister it to one another, as good stewards of the manifold grace of God" (1 Pet. 4:10). Our spiritual gifts work to encourage those around us. We minister to one another. It's not about being happy or positive or upbeat. It's about showing up and allowing the Holy Spirit to use those gifts He's placed inside of you to bless and serve others. Paul writing to the Romans remarked that he was excited to be in person with them soon. Why? "That I may be encouraged together with you **by the mutual faith both of you and me**." (Rom. 1:12, emphasis added)

You may be thinking, *Well it wasn't encouraging when I was there!* And that may be true, though it grieves my heart to hear the church has hurt you. The church—sinners who've recognized their need for a Savior—is not yet perfected. The Bible says, "if one member suffers, all the members suffer with it; or if one member is honored, all the members rejoice with it. Now you are the body of Christ, and members individually" (1 Cor. 12:26-27). It's true whether we're together or apart. When you became a follower of Jesus Christ, you became part of His body. And when one part of the body suffers, we all suffer. But God is still faithful. He wants to draw you to a place where you can feel safe with other believers and find the healing you need. King Solomon wrote, "Though one may be overpowered by another, two can withstand him. And a threefold cord is not quickly broken" (Eccl. 4:12). We are better together. Stronger together. Encouraged together.

You may feel you can't help anyone else. Things are too hard, too difficult for you right now. You've got the weight of the world on your shoulders. *How can I possibly help anyone else? I'm barely keeping myself together! When this pain goes away, then I'll start serving and reaching out to others.* But it's possible the situation you're in will never pass. Waiting until the pain leaves makes you vulnerable to becoming self-absorbed and self-centered. It will smother your faith. Paul, writing to the church in Corinth, said God "comforts us in all our tribulation, **that we may be able to comfort those who are in any trouble**, with the comfort with which we ourselves are comforted by God" (2 Cor. 1:4, emphasis added).

When you're open to the work of the Holy Spirit, He will use you to comfort others in the same way He has comforted you. And sometimes, He comforts you as you grab the hand of someone who's hurting and take them with you to the throne room of God. "**Let us** therefore come boldly to the throne of grace, that **we** may obtain mercy and find grace to help in time of need" (Heb. 4:16, emphasis added).

Bearing Each Other's Burdens

In the book of Galatians, Paul encourages us to share each other's burdens. "Brethren, if a man is overtaken in any trespass, you who are spiritual restore such a one in a spirit of gentleness, considering yourself lest you also be tempted. **Bear one another's burdens, and so fulfill the law of Christ**" (Gal. 6:1-2, emphasis added). When Paul encourages us to share each other's burdens, the word he's using means "heaviness, weight, trouble."[19] But it also means "anything pressing on one physically." Think of someone who's been punched in the gut or had the wind knocked out of them. It feels like you can't breathe. All you're doing is gasping for air. You've been reduced to one thing—the next breath. This is the type of burden Paul is talking about. When life hits you like that, you're in crisis mode.

God calls us to come alongside people in crisis mode to help bear the burdens they are carrying. This is essentially what we're doing when we as a church send teams of people, or money, to places that need relief. Places hit by tragedies of weather or other disasters. We are helping to bear their burdens. We can help share their burdens through relief teams—people on the ground to comfort those who have been afflicted; providing for physical needs through care packages, and resources; and by giving financially to other groups who may be in a better position to minister to those affected by the tragedy.

But Paul isn't simply talking about tragedies like hurricanes, hunger, or shootings. He's also talking about each of us coming alongside others who've been hit hard by life, and helping them bear their burden. Coming alongside people in our family, our neighborhood, our kids' schools, and our church. We do this by being physically present and available for them in their time of need, by praying for them and with them, and perhaps by providing childcare or a warm meal. And sometimes, we can share their burdens by helping them out financially.

Just a few verses later in Galatians, Paul writes, "For each one shall bear his own load" (Gal. 6:5). This almost sounds like a contradiction to his earlier exhortation to share one another's burdens, doesn't it? But Paul uses different words to describe *burdens* and *load*. The word Paul uses for *load*[20] references "something carried," like a soldier's pack.[21] It holds the necessities for the mission the soldier is on. Much like when we're taking our kids on a road trip, we might give them a backpack with just a teddy bear and their favorite snack in it—just the necessities. We carry the rest for them. But for our teenager, he carries all of his things in his backpack. We expect him to carry his own load. Similarly, as believers we are each to carry our own load. We each need to take responsibility for our lives. We aren't to be irresponsible, expecting others to take on responsibilities that should be ours.

At times, we are so consumed with our own troubles, or so desperate to get others to help carry our load—we miss out on the blessing of sharing in the burdens of others. There are those around us who really need our help. We need to be responsible as believers to carry our own load and keep our spiritual eyes open so we can see others who need our help when the Holy Spirit prompts us. We need to reject the attitude of entitlement that so easily creeps in when we are suffering or discouraged. When we begin to think we are owed something. That God owes us or the world owes us. They don't. In fact, there's nothing you could have done to earn your way into heaven. The price of your salvation was costly. It was a gift of love, mercy, and grace. The gift of our salvation motivates us to keep going even through hard times.

God often chooses our weakness and vulnerability to reveal His glory. Paul wrote of his suffering:

> "Concerning this thing I pleaded with the Lord three times that it might depart from me. And He said to me, "My grace is sufficient for you, for My strength is made perfect in weakness." Therefore most gladly I will rather boast in my infirmities, that the power of Christ may rest upon me. Therefore I take pleasure in infirmities, in reproaches, in needs, in persecutions, in distresses, for Christ's sake. For when I am weak, then I am strong." (2 Cor. 12:8-10)

We don't need to be ashamed of the places we've found ourselves. God wants to use you to reveal His glory, and He wants to use His people to reveal His glory and to comfort to You.

Come To Me

Jesus said, "Come to Me, all you who labor and are heavy laden, and I will give you rest. Take My yoke upon you and learn from Me, for I am gentle and lowly in heart, and you will find rest for your souls. For My yoke is easy and My burden is light" (Matt. 11:28-30). In the times of Jesus, a yoke—a kind of harness of wood—would hitch two animals together to carry a load; a heavy cart or some other piece of farming equipment. A yoke was also used to train a younger animal how to carry the load. In yoking two animals together, the older, experienced animal would carry the full weight of the load, while the younger animal would learn to carry the yoke. That's what makes the call of Jesus to take His yoke so powerful for us as believers. Jesus invites us into His rest, to walk alongside Him, yoked together with Him, as He carries the load for us.

The Bible declares Jesus willingly yoked Himself together with us in our humanity and carried the full weight of our sin all the way to the cross. He has lifted the weight of sin and suffering from our shoulders and offers to us the lightness and freedom of His sinlessness in return. This transfer is literal.

"For by one offering He has perfected forever those who are being sanctified. But the Holy Spirit also witnesses to us; for after He had said before, 'This is the covenant that I will make with them after those days, says the Lord: I will put My laws into their hearts, and in their minds I will write them,' then He adds, 'Their sins and their lawless deeds I will remember no more.' Now where there is remission of these, there is no longer an offering for sin." (Heb. 10:14-18)

The biblical term for this transfer is atonement. It's the means by which we are made holy. Here's how the dictionary defines atonement, "the reconciliation of God and humankind through the sacrificial death of Jesus Christ."[22]

In a particularly vulnerable moment in Moses' life, he said to the Lord—If You don't go with us, if You don't lead us to the Promised Land, I'm not going. And the Lord responded, "My Presence will go with you, and I will give you rest" (Exod. 33:14). But Moses persisted, wanting proof he wouldn't be left alone, that God would keep His promise. "'Please, show me Your glory.' Then He said, 'I will make all My goodness pass before you, and I will proclaim the name of the Lord before you. I will be gracious to whom I will be gracious, and I will have compassion on whom I will have compassion'" (Exod. 33:18-19). The word in the original Hebrew translated as "the Lord" here is *Jehovah*. It means "the existing One."[23] It comes from the root *hayah*, meaning "to be, to exist, to abide, to stand, to accompany."[24] There is so much beauty and depth to this name of God, but as it relates to our biblical study through suffering, it means—*I Am* what you need. *I Am* Rest. *I Am* Freedom. *I Am* with you.

For Joseph, *I Am* the One who works all things together for good.

For Hannah, *I Am* the God who hears.

For Abraham, *I Am* the Lord who provides.

For Paul, *I Am* the God of second chances.

For Jeremiah, *I Am* the Potter who forms your life.

For the disciples, *I Am* Peace in the midst of your storm.

For Naomi, *I Am* your Provision, the House of Bread

For Jacob, *I Am* for you, not against you.

God is the great *I Am*. In the midst of your suffering, in the midst of your brokenness, in the midst of your pain, and in the midst of your tragedy, He is becoming exactly what you need. He invites each of us to come to Him through His Son Jesus, and to transfer our sins, our guilt, and our shame for His purity, love, hope, and freedom. His promise is that when you enter His rest, when you yoke yourself together with Him, you will receive His Presence and His peace as you endure suffering. The peace that comes in knowing you are forgiven. The confidence that comes from knowing God is for you, not against you. The hope that God is working all these things together for your good and His glory.

> *"For God did not appoint us to wrath, but to obtain salvation through our Lord Jesus Christ, who died for us, that whether we wake or sleep, we should live together with Him. Therefore comfort each other and edify one another, just as you also are doing."* (1 Thess. 5:9-11)

CHAPTER 11

MORE THAN CONQUERORS

Years ago, two armies stood prepared for battle along the edges of the Valley of Elah. But they weren't fighting. Instead, both armies watched in amazement as a small teenage boy ran into the valley toward a giant—a mighty warrior—armed with only a slingshot and a small pouch of stones. The boy's name was David. His opponent, the giant Goliath, was over nine feet tall. His armor alone weighed 125 pounds; the iron tip of his spear, fifteen pounds. He had an additional man who went before him carrying his shield.

Before David ran out toward the giant, the Israeli and Philistine armies had stood at an impasse for forty days. Waiting. Each day, Goliath walked into the valley and challenged the Israelites to send a man out to fight him. And each day, the men of Israel would wait. *Would anyone accept his challenge? Who would dare fight a giant?* As Goliath strutted into the valley, he mocked and taunted them. "When Saul and all Israel heard these words of the Philistine, they were dismayed and greatly afraid" (1 Sam. 17:11). No one moved. The Hebrew word translated here as "dismayed," means much more than simply afraid. It means, "shattered, terrified, or broken."[25]

Imagine each day coming to the valley and hoping something would change. Hoping something would happen. Hoping God would intervene. Surely, God heard this man mock and taunt His people?

But each day was the same. Nothing changed. No one moved. The giant stood firm and repeated his challenge. No one dared fight him. After forty days, I'm sure they'd lost what little hope they had. They had been under this intense attack for over a month. Just the sound of his voice made their blood pressure sky-rocket and sent their knees shaking. *How will this end? We've lost all hope. How soon until he kills us all?*

They were shattered. Broken. Undone.

Faithful in the Waiting

Long periods of suffering are difficult to endure, especially when there is no end in sight. These times of waiting often bring depression, doubt, and discouragement. Like the Israelites, we wonder where God is in our suffering. We wonder how much longer we can endure. Perhaps you, like me, have received the well-intentioned and yet painful encouragement, "Don't worry! God won't give you more than you can handle!" *Really?* It can be hard to receive truth when we're hurting. But it's simply not true that God will never give you more than you can handle. The sentiment is taken from one of Paul's letters to the Corinthian church: "but God is faithful, who will not allow you to be tempted beyond what you are able, but with the temptation will also make the way of escape, that you may be able to bear it" (1 Cor. 10:13).

The problem is, we've misapplied the verse. Paul isn't telling us God will never give us more than we can handle, or conversely, we will be able to handle every situation God sends our way. That's nonsense. If we could, why would we need to rely on God? Why would we need a way of escape? Think of our sins! We've proved over and over again we can't handle it! No, the Bible is telling us— *God is faithful. God is for you.* When you find yourself in a situation that is more than you can handle (and you will), God will meet you there and provide the way of escape.

In Psalm 73, the psalmist Asaph wrote, "Truly God is good to Israel, to such as are pure in heart. But as for me, my feet had almost stumbled; my steps had nearly slipped" (Ps. 73:1-2). Asaph was falling into a deep pit of despair. Just like the army of Israel, his eyes were fixed on the giant—the overwhelming circumstances of his life. He couldn't understand where God was in it all. He had the wrong perspective. It's not until verse 17 that we see his thinking begin to change: "**Until** I went into the sanctuary of God; **Then** I understood their end." (Ps. 73:17, emphasis added)

Until I went into Your sanctuary. *Then* I understood.

Isn't it amazing how we can enter into God's sanctuary completely depressed and leave encouraged when nothing about our situation has changed? Asaph's perspective changed when He entered into God's sanctuary—the meeting place of God's people. Our faith increases and our perspective changes when we—together with God's people—remind ourselves of who God is, and who He says we are. This is the power of faith; God's gift to us.

In every biblical account of suffering we've studied together, they've found themselves in an impossible situation. They had some insurmountable obstacle to overcome. Something they couldn't possibly handle on their own. Your own personal story has, I'm sure, been beyond your ability to endure at times. But God is faithful. He has not forgotten you. Remind yourself of who God is, and of who He says you are.

"Therefore, brethren, having boldness to enter the Holiest by the blood of Jesus, by a new and living way which He consecrated for us, through the veil, that is, His flesh, and having a High Priest over the house of God, **let us draw near with a true heart in full assurance of faith,** having our hearts sprinkled from an evil conscience and our bodies washed with pure water. Let us hold fast the confession of our hope without wavering, for He who promised is faithful." (Heb. 10:19-23, emphasis added)

God is in the waiting. He can be trusted to keep His promises.

The Battle Belongs to the Lord

As the youngest of Jesse's eight sons, David stayed back to help his father with the sheep. He was only a teenager. But some time later, Jesse sent David to visit his brothers on the battlefield and bring them supplies. David arrived to find his brothers and all of the other soldiers cowering along the edges of the valley. Just then, Goliath came out shouting his usual insults. By this time, the reward for anyone who killed Goliath had grown to include a large sum of money *and* marriage to the king's daughter *and* lifetime tax-exempt status for his entire family. That's some reward! But no one was biting. That's how big the giant was.

David heard Goliath's mockery and asked, "What shall be done for the man who kills this Philistine and takes away the reproach from Israel? For who is this uncircumcised Philistine, that he should defy the armies of the living God?" (1 Sam. 17:26) When David's brothers heard this, they were angry and told him to get lost. But King Saul was so desperate, he sent for David immediately. "Then David said to Saul, 'Let no man's heart fail because of him; your servant will go and fight with this Philistine'" (1 Sam. 17:32). Had David not seen Goliath? Did he not know Goliath was an experienced warrior? Apparently, Saul was wondering the same thing.

> "And Saul said to David, 'You are not able to go against this Philistine to fight with him; for you are a youth, and he a man of war from his youth.'" (1 Sam. 17:33)

But David persisted.

> "'Your servant used to keep his father's sheep, and when a lion or a bear came and took a lamb out of the flock, I went out after it and struck it, and delivered the lamb from its mouth; and when it arose against me, I caught it by its beard, and struck and killed it. Your servant

has killed both lion and bear; and this uncircumcised Philistine will be like one of them, seeing he has defied the armies of the living God.' Moreover David said, 'The Lord, who delivered me from the paw of the lion and from the paw of the bear, He will deliver me from the hand of this Philistine.'" (1 Sam. 17:34-37)

Humanly speaking, the odds were against David. His enemy was a giant, an experienced warrior from his youth. David was a shepherd boy. But David didn't let the naysayers deter him. When Saul tried to give David his armor, David didn't let that weigh him down either. In fact, he chose to face Goliath armed only with five smooth stones and a sling. When Goliath saw David, Goliath disdained him. He had no respect for David at all. "'Am I a dog, that you come to me with sticks?' And the Philistine cursed David by his gods. And the Philistine said to David, 'Come to me, and I will give your flesh to the birds of the air and the beasts of the field!'" (I Sam. 17:43-44)

We too have a real enemy—the devil. Much like Goliath, he taunts, mocks, and encourages us to fight him one on one. Our enemy knows the moment we enter into the battle in our flesh—with our own resources; with sword and spear; with words and emails; with revenge and bitterness—he's won. The apostle Paul wrote, "For we do not wrestle against flesh and blood, but against principalities, against powers, against the rulers of the darkness of this age, against spiritual hosts of wickedness in the heavenly places" (Eph. 6:12).

"Then David said to the Philistine, 'You come to me with a sword, with a spear, and with a javelin. But I come to you in the name of the Lord of hosts, the God of the armies of Israel, whom you have defied. This day the Lord will deliver you into my hand, and I will strike you and take your head from you. And this day I will give the carcasses of the camp of the Philistines to the birds of the air and the wild beasts of the earth, that all the earth may know that there is a God in Israel. Then all this assembly shall know that the Lord does not save with sword and spear; for the battle is the Lord's, and He will give you into our hands.'" (I Sam. 17:45-47)

David entered the battlefield in the name of the Lord. In the biblical context, the name represented the totality of the person. David wasn't fighting in his own strength, his own resources, or his own power—he entered the battle with all of the resources, power, character, and nature of His God. Yahweh. Jehovah. The Becoming One. The God who becomes exactly what you need in the moment. "For though we walk in the flesh, we do not war according to the flesh. For the weapons of our warfare are not carnal but mighty in God for pulling down strongholds." (2 Cor. 10:3-4a)

David was armed with God's mighty weapons—faith, prayer, and praise. David knew who God was, and he knew who he was in God. He had a testimony, a history of God's faithfulness which gave him the boldness and courage to praise God while facing his enemy. This is the same courage and boldness God has for each one of us—your trials and difficulties, your stories of suffering—are your testimony. Your history with God. They are the proof that God is for you. He has delivered you in the past, and He will do it again. "Jesus Christ is the same yesterday, today, and forever" (Heb. 13:8). The same God who protected David from the mouths of the lion and the bear is with you today.

"So it was, when the Philistine arose and came and drew near to meet David, that David hurried and ran toward the army to meet the Philistine. Then David put his hand in his bag and took out a stone; and he slung it and struck the Philistine in his forehead, so that the stone sank into his forehead, and he fell on his face to the earth. So David prevailed over the Philistine with a sling and a stone, and struck the Philistine and killed him. But there was no sword in the hand of David. Therefore David ran and stood over the Philistine, took his sword and drew it out of its sheath and killed him, and cut off his head with it. And when the Philistines saw that their champion was dead, they fled." (1 Sam. 17:48-51)

The Sounds of Praise

In 2 Chronicles 20, Jehoshaphat King of Judah also found himself faced with a giant. Three armies had banded themselves together and declared war on the nation of Israel. They were already marching out against him by the time Jehoshaphat received the news. The Bible says he was afraid but interestingly, it's not the same word used for how the army of Israel felt when they saw Goliath. Jehoshaphat was not yet broken. "And Jehoshaphat feared, and set himself to seek the Lord, and proclaimed a fast throughout all Judah. So Judah gathered together to ask help from the Lord; and from all the cities of Judah they came to seek the Lord." (2 Chron. 20:3-4)

As the people, along with their families and children, came together and stood before the Lord in Jerusalem—Jehoshaphat began to pray. Then, *as they stood before the Lord*, the Spirit of the Lord came upon one of the men standing there.

"Listen, all you of Judah and you inhabitants of Jerusalem, and you, King Jehoshaphat! Thus says the Lord to you: 'Do not be afraid nor dismayed because of this great multitude, for the battle is not yours, but God's. Tomorrow go down against them. They will surely come up by the Ascent of Ziz, and you will find them at the end of the brook before the Wilderness of Jeruel. You will not need to fight in this battle. Position yourselves, stand still and see the salvation of the Lord, who is with you, O Judah and Jerusalem!' Do not fear or be dismayed; tomorrow go out against them, for the Lord is with you." (2 Chron. 20: 15-17)

In response to this word from God, King Jehoshaphat, along with all the people, bowed their faces low to the ground and worshipped the Lord. Then members of the worship team stood to praise the Lord. It must have been an incredible moment.

But what amazes me even more is what happened the next day. During times of deep distress, some of us may go into God's sanctuary and experience His presence. We may even feel encouraged, strengthened, and leave with a weight lifted. But then, it's the next day—and we're not sure what we experienced. Was it a feeling? Was it God? We don't know. We so often have less faith on the second day. But not so with King Jehoshaphat and the people of Israel.

> "So they rose early in the morning and went out into the Wilderness of Tekoa; and as they went out, Jehoshaphat stood and said, 'Hear me, O Judah and you inhabitants of Jerusalem: Believe in the Lord your God, and you shall be established; believe His prophets, and you shall prosper.' **And when he had consulted with the people, he appointed those who should sing to the Lord, and who should praise the beauty of holiness, as they went out before the army and were saying:** 'Praise the Lord, for His mercy endures forever.'" (2 Chron. 20:20-21, emphasis added)

Imagine being part of the choir when King Jehoshaphat appointed you to walk onto the battlefield *ahead of the army*. They were only armed with their instruments as they walked out before three armies. These weren't the commands of a delusional king. Notice, he consulted with the people. They were in agreement on their plan to trust God and send the choir out first, worshipping and praising God. And God gave them the victory.

"Now when they began to sing and to praise, the Lord set ambushes against the people of Ammon, Moab, and Mount Seir, who had come against Judah; and they were defeated." (2 Chron. 20:22)

The armies and choirs of Israel watched as their enemies destroyed each other. The Bible says afterward they went out to collect the plunder and found so many valuables it took them three days to collect everything. "And on the fourth day they assembled in the Valley of Berachah, for there they blessed the Lord; therefore the name of that place was called The Valley of Berachah until this day." (2 Chron. 20:26)

Berakah means "blessing."[26] The place of the battle became the place of blessing.

One of the reasons it's so important for us to run into God's sanctuary during times of distress, or to connect with God's people when we are in distress is because the place of connection becomes our place of victory. Our place of healing. Jesus said, "For where two or three are gathered together in My name, I am there in the midst of them" (Matt. 18:20). Not only does God meet with us when we come together in His name, but as with King Jehoshaphat, He quite often speaks to us through other believers gathered together with us. Someone shares a verse or a testimony which brings comfort. Someone else sings a hymn or a psalm and we leave uplifted and encouraged.

We find healing, strength, power, hope, faith, encouragement and so much more only in the name of Jesus. It's not a feeling. It's faith.

"For whatever is born of God overcomes the world. And this is the victory that has overcome the world—our faith." (I John 5:4)

Overwhelming Victory

"Yet in all these things we are more than conquerors through Him who loved us. For I am persuaded that neither death nor life, nor angels nor principalities nor powers, nor things present nor things to come, nor height nor depth, nor any other created thing, shall be able to separate us from the love of God which is in Christ Jesus our Lord." (Rom. 8:37-38)

Friend, you already have the victory in Jesus Christ. You may not see the fruit of the victory right now, you may not yet be holding Goliath's head in your hand, or collecting the spoils of the battle, but you have already won. Jesus was victorious over sin and death and He shares His victory with you. Nothing can separate you from God's love. There's nothing you've done or could ever do that will separate you from His love. That's how strong His love for you is. Jesus said, "And do not fear those who kill the body but cannot kill the soul. But rather fear Him who is able to destroy both soul and body in hell." (Matt. 10:28)

Many of you have been living as though God is against you, as if He is your adversary. God is for you. It's sin that has separated you and put you at enmity with Him. God is not against you. In fact, God has made every way possible to remedy the problem of your sin. He made a way for you to be at peace with Him—His Son, Jesus. The blood of Jesus is the payment for your sins. His life, perfect—exchanged for your life, imperfect. God's not waiting to punish you because you failed. Your sins have been washed away by the blood of Jesus. God is no longer your enemy. The apostle John wrote, "You are of God, little children, and have overcome them, because He who is in you is greater than he who is in the world" (1 John 4:4).

Like Abraham, like Hannah, like Joseph, like Ruth and Naomi— God is for you. He is already working these things together for your good and His glory. In the midst of your suffering, your trials, and tragedies, He has provided Himself—the sacrifice for your sins, the comfort for your sorrows, the answer to your prayers, the solution to your problems. In spite of these things, overwhelming victory is ours in Christ Jesus.

"These things I have spoken to you, that in Me you may have peace. In the world you will have tribulation; but be of good cheer, I have overcome the world."

-Jesus (John 16:33)

"What then shall we say to these things? If God is for us, who can be against us? He who did not spare His own Son, but delivered Him up for us all, how shall He not with Him also freely give us all things? Who shall bring a charge against God's elect? It is God who justifies. Who is he who condemns? It is Christ who died, and furthermore is also risen, who is even at the right hand of God, who also makes intercession for us. Who shall separate us from the love of Christ? Shall tribulation, or distress, or persecution, or famine, or nakedness, or peril, or sword? As it is written: 'For Your sake we are killed all day long; we are accounted as sheep for the slaughter.' Yet in all these things we are more than conquerors through Him who loved us. For I am persuaded that neither death nor life, nor angels nor principalities nor powers, nor things present nor things to come, nor height nor depth, nor any other created thing, shall be able to separate us from the love of God which is in Christ Jesus our Lord." (Rom. 8:31-39)

CONCLUSION

My hope for you is that you have found some encouragement, some peace with God, as you've journeyed through this biblical theology of suffering—God's help for our troubled hearts.

My own family's journey of walking through grief and loss did not end with an overnight healing. We struggled through grief and doubt with the help of God and other believers. We still bear the scars of that tragic day. But I am reminded our Savior also still bears the scars of His suffering here on earth. His hands and feet still hold the marks of the nails that bore Him through. His side is marked where the soldiers pierced Him as He hung on the cross—the place where blood mixed with water poured out. His wounding has become our healing. And so too, our wounding becomes a place of His healing in our lives. The Potter touches the very place where sin has marred us with His own nail scarred hands.

"Come, and let us return to the Lord; for He has torn, but He will heal us; He has stricken, but He will bind us up. After two days He will revive us; on the third day He will raise us up, that we may live in His sight. Let us know, let us pursue the knowledge of the Lord. His going forth is established as the morning; He will come to us like the rain, like the latter and former rain to the earth." (Hosea 6:1-3)

Not one of us will leave this planet unscathed from the scars and effects of sin. Some may hide it better than others, but make no mistake—we all suffer. The question remains—*Will you trust God and surrender your life to Him?*

He really is working all things together for your good and His glory. He loves you.

Be sober, be vigilant; because your adversary the devil walks about like a roaring lion, seeking whom he may devour. Resist him, steadfast in the faith, knowing that the same sufferings are experienced by your brotherhood in the world. But may the God of all grace, who called us to His eternal glory by Christ Jesus, after you have suffered a while, perfect, establish, strengthen, and settle you. To Him be the glory and the dominion forever and ever. Amen. (1 Peter 5:8-11)

NOTES

CHAPTER 4

1. "G5281 - hypomonē - Strong's Greek Lexicon (KJV)." Blue Letter Bible. Accessed 24 Jul, 2020. https://www.blueletterbible.org//lang/lexicon/lexicon.cfm?strongs=G5281&t=KJV

2. "G5259 - hypo - Strong's Greek Lexicon (KJV)." Blue Letter Bible. Accessed 4 Aug, 2020. https://www.blueletterbible.org//lang/lexicon/lexicon.cfm?strongs=G5259&t=KJV

3. "G3306 - menō - Strong's Greek Lexicon (KJV)." Blue Letter Bible. Accessed 4 Aug, 2020. https://www.blueletterbible.org//lang/lexicon/lexicon.cfm?strongs=G3306&t=KJV

4. William Barclay, The Gospel of Matthew Volume Two, (Kentucky, Saint Andrew Press, 2001), 424.

5. David Guzik, "Enduring Word Bible Commentary 2 Corinthians Chapter 4", Enduring Word, accessed August 9, 2019 https://enduringword.com/bible-commentary/2-corinthians-4/

CHAPTER 5

6. "G3049 - logizomai - Strong's Greek Lexicon (NKJV)." Blue Letter Bible. Accessed 25 Jul, 2020. https://www.blueletterbible.org//lang/lexicon/lexicon.cfm?strongs=G3049&t=NKJV

CHAPTER 6

7. "H7843 - shachath - Strong's Hebrew Lexicon (NKJV)." Blue Letter Bible. Accessed 25 Jul, 2020. https://www.blueletterbible.org//lang/lexicon/lexicon.cfm?strongs=H7843&t=NKJV

8. "G2347 - thlipsis - Strong's Greek Lexicon (NKJV)." Blue Letter Bible. Accessed 25 Jul, 2020. https://www.blueletterbible.org//lang/lexicon/lexicon.cfm?strongs=G2347&t=NKJV

9. "G5278 - hypomenō - Strong's Greek Lexicon (KJV)." Blue Letter Bible. Accessed 4 Aug, 2020. https://www.blueletterbible.org//lang/lexicon/lexicon.cfm?strongs=G5278&t=KJV

CHAPTER 8

10. "H458 - 'Eliymelek - Strong's Hebrew Lexicon (KJV)." Blue Letter Bible. Accessed 5 Aug, 2020. https://www.blueletterbible.org//lang/lexicon/lexicon.cfm?strongs=H458&t=KJV

11. "H5281 - No`omiy - Strong's Hebrew Lexicon (KJV)." Blue Letter Bible. Accessed 5 Aug, 2020. https://www.blueletterbible.org//lang/lexicon/lexicon.cfm?strongs=H5281&t=KJV

12. "H1035 - Beyth Lechem - Strong's Hebrew Lexicon (KJV)." Blue Letter Bible. Accessed 5 Aug, 2020. https://www.blueletterbible.org//lang/lexicon/lexicon.cfm?strongs=H1035&t=KJV

13. "H6204 - `Orpah - Strong's Hebrew Lexicon (KJV)." Blue Letter Bible. Accessed 5 Aug, 2020. https://www.blueletterbible.org//lang/lexicon/lexicon.cfm?Strongs=H6204&t=KJV

14. "H7327 - Ruwth - Strong's Hebrew Lexicon (KJV)." Blue Letter Bible. Accessed 5 Aug, 2020. https://www.blueletterbible.org//lang/lexicon/lexicon.cfm?Strongs=H7327&t=KJV

15. Warren W. Wiersbe, Be Committed (Ruth & Esther): Doing God's Will Whatever the Cost (Colorado Springs, CO: David C Cook, 2008.)

16. "H4755 - Mara' - Strong's Hebrew Lexicon (KJV)." Blue Letter Bible. Accessed 5 Aug, 2020. https://www.blueletterbible.org//lang/lexicon/lexicon.cfm?Strongs=H4755&t=KJV

CHAPTER 9

17. "H3290 - Ya`aqob - Strong's Hebrew Lexicon (KJV)." Blue Letter Bible. Accessed 5 Aug, 2020. https://www.blueletterbible.org//lang/lexicon/lexicon.cfm?Strongs=H3290&t=KJV

18. Merriam-Webster.com Dictionary, s.v. "supplant," accessed August 13, 2020, https://www.merriam-webster.com/dictionary/supplant.

CHAPTER 10

19. "G922 - baros - Strong's Greek Lexicon (KJV)." Blue Letter Bible. Accessed 10 Aug, 2020. https://www.blueletterbible.org//lang/lexicon/lexicon.cfm?Strongs=G922&t=KJV

20. "G5413 - phortion - Strong's Greek Lexicon (KJV)." Blue Letter Bible. Accessed 14 Aug, 2020. https://www.blueletterbible.org//lang/lexicon/lexicon.cfm?Strongs=G5413&t=KJV

21. Vine, W. "Burden, Burdened, Burdensome - Vine's Expository Dictionary of New Testament Words." Blue Letter Bible. Last Modified 24 Jun, 1996. https://www.blueletterbible.org/search/dictionary/viewtopic.cfm

22. "atonement." Merriam-Webster.com. 2019. https://www.merriam-webster.com (10 December 2019).

23. "H3068 - Yehovah - Strong's Hebrew Lexicon (NKJV)." Blue Letter Bible. Accessed 12 Aug, 2020. https://www.blueletterbible.org//lang/lexicon/lexicon.cfm?Strongs=H3068&t=NKJV

24. "H1961 - hayah - Strong's Hebrew Lexicon (NKJV)." Blue Letter Bible. Accessed 12 Aug, 2020. https://www.blueletterbible.org//lang/lexicon/lexicon.cfm?Strongs=H1961&t=NKJV

CHAPTER 11

25. "H2865 - chathath - Strong's Hebrew Lexicon (NKJV)." Blue Letter Bible. Accessed 12 Aug, 2020. https://www.blueletterbible.org//lang/lexicon/lexicon.cfm?Strongs=H2865&t=NKJV

26. "H1294 - Berakah - Strong's Hebrew Lexicon (NKJV)." Blue Letter Bible. Accessed 12 Aug, 2020. https://www.blueletterbible.org//lang/lexicon/lexicon.cfm?Strongs=H1294&t=NKJV

ADDITIONAL RESOURCES

We have provided additional resources for you to help you with what you are going through right now, whether you're walking through grief and loss, working through the aftermath of terrorism, or would like more information on how to encourage someone you love. All those details, as well as the original teaching series, Help for Troubled Hearts, from which this book originated from can be found at:

www.helpforthetroubledheart.com

You can connect with Ed Taylor via his website www.edtaylor.org, or email him directly ed@edtaylor.org.

ABOUNDING GRACE
MEDIA GROUP™